Nothing Gold Can Stay

Nature's first green is gold,
Her hardest hue to hold.
Her first leaf's a flower;
But only so an hour.
Then leaf subsides to leaf.
So Eden sank to grief,
So dawn goes down to day.
Nothing gold can stay.
—Robert Frost

Nothing Gold Can Stay

A Memoir

Walter Sullivan

University of Missouri Press   Columbia and London

Copyright © 2006 by
The Curators of the University of Missouri
University of Missouri Press, Columbia, Missouri 65201
Printed and bound in the United States of America
All rights reserved
5   4   3   2   1   10   09   08   07   06

Library of Congress Cataloging-in-Publication Data

Sullivan, Walter, 1924–
    Nothing gold can stay : a memoir / Walter Sullivan.
        p.   cm.
    ISBN-13: 978-0-8262-1631-1 (alk. paper)
    ISBN-10: 0-8262-1631-5 (alk. paper)
    1. Sullivan, Walter, 1924–   2. English philology—Study and
teaching—Tennessee—Nashville.   3. Novelists, American—20th
century—Biography.   4. English teachers—United States—Biography.
5. Vanderbilt University—Faculty—Biography.   I. Title.
    PS3569.U3593Z47   2005
    813'.54—dc22   2005019701

♾™ This paper meets the requirements of the
American National Standard for Permanence of Paper
for Printed Library Materials, Z39.48, 1984.

Designer: Jennifer Cropp
Typesetter: Phoenix Type, Inc.
Printer and binder: The Maple-Vail Book Manufacturing Group
Typefaces: Minion and Caslon

For those who come after

Contents

Acknowledgments

I owe profound thanks to more people than I have space to list here: to my wife, Jane, who has read my manuscripts and commented on them for more than fifty years; to Pam and her husband, Gordon Chenery, who urged me to undertake this memoir; to Larry and his wife, Molly, whose questions reminded me of scenes that belonged in the narrative; to John, for suggesting ways that my writing could be improved; to the grandchildren—Taylor, Christopher, and Anne Laurence Chenery; Elizabeth, Will, and Kate Sullivan—for being willing to listen to the stories told by a garrulous old man.

I owe an unpayable debt to my friends. Louis Rubin and the late Lewis Simpson both published some of my earliest work. I was fortunate to appear on literary programs with them and to be blessed by their company in many different places and in many ways. George Core comes third only because he is younger than the rest of us. I am grateful to him for reading and editing my manuscripts, including this one. For their friendship, their advice, their work, and the examples of their lives, I thank George Garrett, Joe Blotner, Elizabeth Spencer, Wendell Berry, Shelby Foote, Madison Jones, Bill Hoffman, Fred Chappell—and many more. Too many of those who helped me and whose friendship warmed me are gone and have left us poorer by their passing: Cleanth Brooks, Peter Taylor, Walker Percy, Robert Penn Warren, Allen Tate, Andrew

Lytle, Donald Davidson, and Donald Davie. I thank my colleagues in academia: Ward Allen and his wife, Peggy, who is also a scholar and writer, and their children, Jerry and Mary and Will and Peter, one Jane's godson, the other mine; Randall Stewart; Jack Aden; Hal Weatherby, who was my student before he was my colleague. Robert Benson and John Glass were also my students, two of many who are still a part of my life.

I was fortunate to have friends outside the academic-literary world: Louise and the late Virgil LeQuire, she a painter, he a physician, whose company Jane and I cherished for half a century; their children, Nancy (our goddaughter), Paul, Lista, and Alan, a sculptor, who joined me— or I joined him—in staying up too late and drinking too much bad Italian wine more than twenty years ago at Bracciano. Judge Henry Denmark Bell and his late wife, Allen, parents of novelist Madison Smartt Bell, with whom we ate and drank and talked and sang through many afternoons and evenings. Maclin Davis, a lawyer, and his late wife, Dot, who were close and loyal friends. Mac and I hunted together, not always successfully. Their daughter, Dee, is our goddaughter; Mac III and Joe were in school with John and Larry.

I thank members of the Fellowship of Southern Writers not only for their friendship and their many acts of kindness to me but also for the work they have done to sustain our literary tradition. They are too many to be named individually here, but they are known in the literary community.

Finally, as is often the case, the last to be thanked are among the most helpful in preparing a book for publication—the professionals who edit our manuscripts and endure our vanities. I thank Jane Lago for taming my barbarisms and sharpening my writing. And I am deeply grateful to Beverly Jarrett, director of the University of Missouri Press, for her interest in this book and her help in developing it. We have worked together before. We have been friends for a long time. I am blessed to have her help and her goodwill. This book, which is hers as well as mine, is better for it.

Nothing Gold Can Stay

Chapter One

A Long Descent

Because my father died three months after I was born, I spent my infancy in a grieving family. In photographs taken after my father's death, my mother wears mourning: a long black dress and a black hat with a veil, although in most pictures the veil is lifted. In one picture, I am standing on the Sullivan headstone at Mount Olivet Cemetery with my mother, still dressed in mourning, standing beside me, her hand on my back in case I should lose my balance. My Sullivan grandmother wore mourning too, and I have a photograph of her with me in her arms, she wearing a dress similar to the dress my mother wore, but no hat, no veil, for we were not at the cemetery but at the house she and my grandfather would lose in the Depression. Every Sunday afternoon, my grandfather and grandmother, "Granddaddy" and "Chigger," and my Aunt Pauline, whom I called "Auntie," would come to where my mother and I lived with my other grandparents, and we would ride to the cemetery. In those days, the mid-1920s, Nashville was not a large city; traffic was light. We made a slow but constant progress from East Nashville to the old entrance at Mount Olivet, through the gates and up the hill past the office that is now a funeral home. We parked on the side of a narrow road and walked to my father's grave, watching our steps, moving carefully around the tombstones.

In the Sullivan plot, there were six spaces: the one where my father lay, one for my mother, Granddaddy said, one for me, and one each for Granddaddy and Chigger and Auntie. When we arrived, we would see at the head of my father's grave a vase of withered flowers, which one of the ladies would replace with fresh flowers that would themselves wither before we returned. Now, after a lifetime of reading books and trying to write them, I see the flowers as a conventional, even trite, image of death, their vulnerability to the passage of time as hackneyed a reminder of the fate of living things as were the graves that surrounded us; but I was too young to consider this, and I believe that my mother and grandparents thought of little except their grief. My mother and father had been married in 1921. They had lived together less than three years before he died. He passed quickly from good health to sickness, contracted peritonitis, and died within a week in that time before the discovery of antibiotics. When he died, my parents had recently bought a house with money borrowed from Granddaddy, which seems ironic in view of Granddaddy's later poverty. But until the stock market crash in 1929 and the Great Depression that followed, Granddaddy and Chigger and Auntie lived comfortably on the money Granddaddy earned as a road contractor.

We made our trips to the cemetery in Granddaddy's automobile, which was blue on the outside and had blue leather upholstery and glass bud vases and a place for a picnic basket and another for golf clubs. Auntie drove. Granddaddy sat beside her. I rode in the backseat between Chigger and my mother. If the car had a heater, the heat it generated was insufficient even for Nashville's mild winters. In cold weather, those of us in the backseat covered ourselves with a lap robe. In summer, we opened the windows as well as the windshield, which was hinged at the top and could be pushed out at the bottom. Sometimes, after we had left the cemetery, we rode around Nashville, and my first encounter with literacy was learning to identify letters on billboards. Chigger told me that I had sharp young eyes, which I took as a just reward for my virtue. Even in our ambience of grief and death, my innocence was unshakable. Granddaddy showed me the first dead man I ever saw, one whom to this day I cannot identify. Was this at a funeral?

A funeral home? A house? I remember only that Granddaddy lifted me up so I could look at Uncle Will, who lay stiller than any person I had seen before; he had a pale face and a white moustache tinged yellow at the edges. Whose uncle was he? To which side of the family did he belong? What degree of consanguinity could he have claimed with me? I never knew. I have only the recollection of his face, disconnected from other memories. Out of context.

The trees at the cemetery were productive. I relished the persimmons that grew not far from my father's grave and were ripened by the frosts of autumn. We collected hickory nuts that Granddaddy cracked—small inside their husks and parsimonious, convoluted as if to protect their meat, which itself was not very tasty. How grisly this seems now, eating the fruit of the trees that were nourished by the bodies of the dead, my father's included. If my mother or grandparents thought of this—and surely they must have—they said nothing. They tidied up the grave, cut the grass with shears, and allowed me to wander among the tombstones, which, like the billboards, helped me to learn to read. A plot next to that of the Sullivans belonged to W. C. "Titsy" Carter. He was not dead, but he had provided a stone for himself in advance, the date of his mortality left blank. Two of Titsy's wives lay on each side of his future grave. My mother, who had never seen Titsy and knew nothing about him except that she had heard that he was married to a third wife, looked with a suspicious eye on Titsy's domestic history. She had no evidence, she had heard no gossip concerning his marriages, and she did not suspect him of felonious conduct; but she did think that Titsy had not been as considerate of his wives as he might have been. "He must have helped drive them to their graves," my mother said. "I can't help believing they would have lived longer if he had been nicer to them."

Although I never saw the victim's grave or even heard his name to remember it, I knew that Granddaddy's brother-in-law, Julian Dye, had killed a man, shot him down on the street in full light of day, but Uncle Julian had never gone to prison. "Why not?" I asked one night when the subject came up at the dinner table. "Because of the unwritten law," Granddaddy said. Chigger and Auntie both nodded knowingly, as if "the unwritten law" was generally understood and applied often. I asked what the unwritten law was, and Granddaddy, who held nothing back, tried to explain it in terms suitable to my ears and in deference to the presence of the ladies. I didn't understand until later and don't fully understand even now. Aunt Lottie, Uncle Julian's wife, who had been named for her and Granddaddy's mother, Charlotte Gower Sullivan, had been—what? pursued? courted? seduced?—by the man Uncle Julian murdered. My mother, who knew the story, was astonished that Granddaddy should have mentioned it. She thought that whatever the circumstances, however innocent Aunt Lottie might have been, any tale that mentioned Aunt Lottie's name should remain untold. Skeletons, she thought, should stay in their closets.

Aunt Lottie and Uncle Julian had three children whom I remember: Willis, named for Aunt Lottie's and Granddaddy's father; Irving; and Virginia. Willis and Irving treated me with rough, masculine affection, but even as young as I was, I sensed that, like Uncle Julian, they were not to be trifled with. When times were good, Uncle Julian, who was also a road contractor, and Granddaddy sometimes worked together, but in the Depression, few roads were built. I don't know what changes took place in Uncle Julian's life, but Granddaddy's fortunes plummeted. I understood only vaguely what was happening. Things disappeared without explanation, small things at first. The pistol Granddaddy would let me touch, but not hold; his billy, made not of wood but of leather with a lead weight on the end, like the gun a relic of his days on the police force. Later the player piano, the pedals of which I could pump if I pulled the bench close, was gone from the entrance hall. My mother noticed that Auntie no longer wore her diamond ring.

At the beginning of the Depression, the marriage of Uncle Leonard, my father's younger brother, to Corine Green failed, and he came to live with Granddaddy and Chigger. I don't remember where he worked in Nashville, but whatever his job was, he lost it. He no longer had his car, although Corine might have taken it when she and their daughter went to live with her parents in Alabama. Without work or any prospect of work, Uncle Leonard went every day to the fire hall down the street and played cards and visited with the firemen. He wanted to be a fireman himself, but so did a thousand other men who were seeking work anywhere they could find it. One afternoon, a house near the fire hall caught fire. Uncle Leonard was the first to see smoke seeping through the cracks around the door and the windows. He raised the alarm and, in doing so, raised his own naive hopes, but his discovery of the fire didn't help him to get a job as a fireman. With no prospects for a job and with Corine pressing him for the alimony and child support the courts had awarded her, he fled to Ohio.

After Uncle Leonard had left Nashville, but before my grandparents lost their house, Grandma, Chigger's mother, Sally Fudge, came to live with them. She was a small woman, short and thin with lean, almost sharp features; until she was bedridden near the end of her life, she stood straight and walked with grace and sat with her long skirts hiding her feet and ankles. In my recollection, her clothes were always gray, often with small, black prints, relics of another age, as she was. She had been born in the Old South, she had lived through the Civil War, she had endured deprivation long before the Great Depression. Auntie frequently spoke sharply to her, but she was kind and patient, and she kept busy visiting the sick and going to funerals. Granddaddy said amiably that she went to the funerals of people she didn't know, which was almost true. She would go to a funeral if she had the slightest acquaintance with any member of the deceased's family. She made the move from my grandparents' house on Charlotte Pike to a small house on Church Street, but by the mid-1930s she was very old, and once she took to her bed, she did not linger. She, too, was buried at Mount Olivet, but next to her husband in a different part of the cemetery from ours.

Granddaddy and Chigger must have been desperate with worry, but whatever they felt they hid from me. We still walked on Saturday nights to the Elite Theater to watch silent films, an inspiration for me to learn to read because nobody, including my mother when I went with her, read the subtitles to my satisfaction. They didn't read them quickly enough, and their renditions lacked passion. I did better when I repeated the lines for my playmates. Granddaddy could have done better too, but he left the reading up to Chigger. Granddaddy was a superb raconteur. I did not realize until years after I had heard most of his stories that although they were based in fact, he gave his imagination free rein. He told of the police chief named Milliron, pronounced fittingly Mill-iron, in keeping with the rough courage that he displayed in Granddaddy's narratives. Apparently Milliron took an active role in police work and confronted many criminals. Granddaddy, who had not been present on most of these occasions, invented dialogue for both parties, lines much superior to those that the cowboys used in the movies. But Granddaddy did not have to root his work in personal experience. One of his best stories was an elaboration or, more than that, a flight of dramatic fancy inspired by an account of star-crossed lovers he read in the newspaper. The bones of the narrative were badly shopworn. A married doctor was in love with a woman other than his wife. He refused to divorce and marry his lover, who in despair or retaliation took bichloride of mercury, a slow but sure poison much talked about in the 1930s. Its proper use was to treat wounds. Unaccountably, it came as a white tablet that was sometimes mistaken for aspirin. Having taken it, by error or otherwise, the patient lingered for days before dying, which gave the doctor and his paramour time for bathetic scenes of love and regret.

My mother told me what she knew about this case. According to the newspapers, the doctor sat beside his dying lover's bed weeping, his tears matched by hers. But reporters were not allowed in the hospital room, and they could not report dialogue that they hadn't heard. Not so with Granddaddy. It was hard to believe that the same person who had devised hard lines for Chief Milliron, threatening miscreants with mayhem and death, could apply his imagination to the doctor's grief to such maudlin effect. The doctor sat as close as he could decently get to the bed. He told the woman that he loved her, but Granddaddy knew instinctively that love scenes are hard to write. The words *I love you* have been spoken so many times by lovers real and fictional that they have no force except for those who speak and hear them. In Granddaddy's tale the doctor felt not only love and sorrow, guilt and regret, but also outrage that the woman should have acted like such a fool. He could hardly ask her why. The answer was that she loved him, and he knew it. After more than seventy years, I cannot reprise Granddaddy's dialogue. The doctor told the woman that she should not have taken the tablet. She apologized for having done so, but she could not resist reminding him of her broken heart. Granddaddy, instinctively once again, maintained the point of view of the doctor whose anger and affection ebbed and flowed, but love and sorrow formed Granddaddy's prevailing theme. He gave a masterful performance.

Finally, the high adventure that Granddaddy longed to shape and elaborate evaded him. My father served in the navy during World War I, and for eight months he was part of the crew of the USS *Sterling*, a destroyer that, according to navy records, patrolled on the Bay of Biscay during most of the war. I do not know what conversations might have occurred between Granddaddy and my father after the armistice. According to relatives on my mother's side who knew him, my father was also a good raconteur, and he too liked to reshape stories and furnish details. Granddaddy wanted to hear something that would expand his repertoire, and, even better, give him new material to recast in dramatic terms and to endow with dialogue. He must have tempted my father greatly. Old sailors, like old soldiers, like to talk, to tell of campaigns and the heroics thereof, the suffering and the bravery and, sometimes, even the comic, but, perhaps more frequently than in stories of mundane existence, the truth is eroded by repetition. In the evolution of their being told, the stories themselves become what is true.

My father brought home from the war a Croix de Guerre, the pin at the top of the ribbon missing, the ribbon frayed, and the sharp end of one of the swords bent. The medal had been awarded to somebody. If Granddaddy could have talked to the man who won it, surely, he would have had material to endure through many tellings, but if my father knew to whom the medal had been given, the knowledge did not come down to me. My mother did not even know where my father had got the medal. A pawn shop? A flea market? A Frenchman down on his luck? But no matter. I expect that when my father was talking to my grandfather, my father must have been tempted to claim the Croix de Guerre, to create a tale of himself that would last both him and Granddaddy for the rest of their lives. He didn't. Granddaddy would have clung to the story if he had. The only medal my father won was the victory medal that was given to everyone who served during that war. But I wonder if once my father didn't yield to temptation. When I was almost grown, Granddaddy referred vaguely to the time that my father's ship had been attacked by a submarine and sunk. I was immediately ready to listen. Here was a new adventure. Had my father told of this imaginary sinking and then backed away from it as Granddaddy did now? If so, like Granddaddy, he must not have been able to bring it off. Any war stories he might have told must have been hopelessly undramatic.

I do not know where my mother and father met, but I would guess at Hume-Fogg High School. He lived in West Nashville, she in East, but at that time Hume-Fogg was the only high school in the city. According to all reports, the teachers there maintained rigid standards. My Uncle

Jim Armstrong, my mother's brother, who made his way in life well enough, failed English in his senior year at Hume-Fogg and did not graduate. I do not know whether my father graduated. His navy record does not give the level of his education. It lists his civilian occupation as "stenographer." After his discharge, he worked at the post office. He helped found the Nashville chapter of the Postal Workers Union. His picture still hangs in the Nashville Labor Temple designating him a pioneer in the labor movement. He was the first president of the Nashville chapter of the union and held that office at the time of his death. Given his position at the post office, he would likely have survived the Great Depression better than men who worked for private companies and saw their jobs disappear.

When my father died in 1924, the economy was flourishing, but six years later, when the Depression began, Chigger and Granddaddy and Auntie had a new reason to mourn his death. Their house on Charlotte Pike was old, built around or perhaps before 1900. It was heated with fireplaces and the bathroom had been added after the house was completed, but the house was commodious and solidly built. There was a large entrance hall where in good times the player piano stood. The parlor, seldom used, was off the entrance hall. It had double sliding doors and lamps with red fringed shades and an uncomfortable Victorian couch facing the fireplace. There were four large bedrooms, a dining room, a kitchen, and a big pantry where, when Uncle Leonard was still around to make it, home brew was stored. The house had two long porches, one at the front and one at the side, and some outbuildings, a woodshed, a small stable where briefly Granddaddy kept a pony he had bought for me to ride when I visited. After dinner, we usually sat in the dining room, and on Saturday nights, when we didn't go to the picture show as we called it then, we listened to the Grand Ole Opry. Most of the performers in those days were gifted amateurs whose traditional music seemed particularly to please Granddaddy. One of the songs went, "'How many biscuits can you eat this morning? How many biscuits can you eat this evening? How many biscuits can you eat?' 'Forty-nine and a ham of meat, this morning for breakfast so soon.'" Another song asked, "Who broke the lock on the hen house door?" Door was pronounced to rhyme with "go." Another was "Eleven cent cotton and forty cent meat. How in the world can a poor man eat?" There were breakdowns such as "Soldiers Joy," and ballads such as "Barbara Allen."

After the pistol and the billy and the player piano and Auntie's diamond ring were gone, Chigger and Granddaddy lost the house. They must have thought, as my mother did, that if my father had not died, he would have helped them. He might not have been able to save their house, but as times worsened, he could have relieved some of their bitter poverty. My mother helped them as much as she could, but her income as a schoolteacher was skimpy. She had me to support, and tuition to pay at Peabody College for Teachers, where every summer she took work toward a degree. Later she became principal of the school where she taught, but even then she had little money to spare. Sometimes, Chigger called my mother and asked for money. Mother always give what she could. Often she gave Chigger money without being asked, but always small amounts, five or ten dollars, enough to keep Chigger and Granddaddy and Auntie fed. But the downward slide of my grandparents' fortunes was uninterrupted, and their luck seemed always to be bad.

Chigger had diabetes, for which she received little treatment. In those hard times, even families with steady incomes were reluctant to consult a doctor. Occasionally my mother would give Chigger money to be treated for her diabetes and later for an injured foot that, because of the diabetes, would not heal. Mostly Chigger was treated as a charity case at the old City Hospital. When I was old enough to drive, I would take her and Auntie to the free clinic. Once I went with them into the waiting room where the uncomfortable benches were crowded with poorly dressed people who were flushed with fever or heavily bandaged or wore a cast on an arm or a leg. The room smelled of hospital disinfectant and sickness, of soiled clothes and perspiration. Chigger and Auntie found seats, but I didn't stay. I went back to our automobile and waited until Chigger was ready to leave.

Chigger had arthritis as well as diabetes, and her arthritis became worse after she broke her hip. Or rather, her hip was broken by the carelessness of a drugstore delivery boy who rode his bicycle on the sidewalk and hit Chigger and knocked her down. Through the days of their deep poverty, they bought me popcorn at the movie; they gave me presents on my birthday and at Christmas. At Christmas, before they lost their house, Granddaddy would cut a cedar tree, set it up in the dining room, and Chigger and Auntie would decorate it with ornaments they had had since long before I was born. There were no lights, but the ornaments sparkled and the tree smelled good and under it a present for me waited. I was happy, foolishly, innocently happy, even as I noticed that from year to year the tree looked less festive. Ornaments were broken, and in that impecunious household they could not be replaced.

Chigger was in bed with her injured hip for what seemed to me to be a long time. Afterward, she walked with a crutch for the rest of her life. As time passed, I visited Chigger and Granddaddy less frequently. I went to Boy Scout meetings on Friday nights. I found my neighborhood friends more interesting than my family. When I did go to see Chigger and Granddaddy, they gave me small amounts of money they couldn't afford to give, and I took what they gave me, thinking only of myself. The Sullivans moved and moved again. Chigger's damaged foot remained unhealed until it became gangrenous and the doctors at the free clinic recommended that the foot be removed. She adamantly declined and once more took to her bed. At that time, she and Granddaddy and Auntie were living on Shelby Avenue. Chigger's bed was in a front room where Auntie nursed her day and night. Like the waiting room at City Hospital, Chigger's room smelled of illness, the odor of her decaying foot never fully masked by those of rubbing alcohol and disinfectant.

During her last illness, I went to see Chigger often. After dinner, I would borrow my mother's car, drive to Shelby Avenue, stay for a while at Chigger's bedside, then go to spend time with my friends. The Sullivans had no phone by means of which my mother could have ascertained my whereabouts, but probably by checking the odometer, or the level of gasoline in the tank, she knew that I was going places other than to see Chigger. One night she hired a taxi and had the driver park near Chigger's house where she could keep her car and me under surveillance. She didn't know that Uncle Leonard, who had left town owing alimony and child support, had come from Ohio to see his dying mother. Although he had been away from Nashville for ten years or more, once he got to Tennessee he was frightened of his shadow. His long absence notwithstanding, he thought that the police would still be searching for him. After his arrival he hurried out of the bus station with his collar turned up and caught his own cab to Shelby Avenue. Until I entered Chigger's room, I didn't know that Uncle Leonard had come. But Auntie and Chigger had assured him that I would take him back to the bus station, which I set out to do. Seeing me leave the house with another man, my mother, angry at me, but proud of having caught me, instructed her driver to follow her car. She intercepted us at the first traffic signal.

Uncle Leonard was terrified. Even though, as Uncle Leonard knew, there were no women on the Nashville police force then, and, in any event, the police did not ordinarily ride in cabs, he was certain that he was going to be arrested. He was fearful beyond coherence. He started to tell me to drive on, and then thought better of it. He sputtered, trying to say something else, but no words left his mouth. He opened the door on his side of the car, but the taxi had stopped on that side, and he was facing my mother, who had left the taxi. He did not recognize her. She did not recognize him. Because he was much older than any of my friends, she was certain that some deep mischief was afoot. I was too young and inexperienced to remain silent and allow this moment to move to its comic conclusion.

"Why, it's Mother," I said.

It was easy to explain to her that Uncle Leonard had spent the day in Nashville visiting his mother. My mother realized that she needed to explain why she had hired a taxi to follow her own car, driven by her own son, who was taking his frightened uncle to the bus station. She tried. "Well," she said. "You see . . ." Then she gave up and attempted to talk of mundane matters to Uncle Leonard, but the fright she had given him had made him incapable of conversation. I wonder now if he didn't feel guilty. Perhaps seeing Nashville had brought back memories of happier days, memories that included his ex-wife and the daughter he had abandoned. At the bus station, he got out quickly, grabbed his bag, and hurried inside as if he still feared that my mother had come to arrest him. My mother and I stopped by to see Chigger on our way home.

I spent the night of Chigger's death at the house on Shelby Avenue. She was in a coma when I arrived. Auntie sat by her bed as she had the night before and many days and nights before that, waiting for what had to come, but not resigned to it. For a long time, Chigger had been sick, feverish, and in pain. She told Auntie that she wanted to die, and she asked Auntie not to help her die, but to release her, to give up her determination that Chigger should live on, day after day, week after week, to be cared for by Auntie, who seemed to be incapable of admitting to herself that Chigger's death was inevitable. Perhaps, at the end, Auntie, exhausted from her long vigil at Chigger's bedside, was no longer capable of willing Chigger to continue to live. More likely, in spite of Auntie's desires, the disease took its course. Chigger died at about three o'clock in the morning.

Auntie, who had been watching Chigger and dozing in her chair, awakened Granddaddy and me. We stood around Chigger's bed as she took a few low-pitched, gurgling breaths, coughed up mucus that ran down her chin, and then breathed no more. Auntie cleaned Chigger's face, shut her eyes, which required no coins to make them stay shut, and tied a strip of cloth under Chigger's chin and over her head, which closed her mouth and held her lips together. Then Auntie kissed her on the forehead and pulled the sheet over her face. Grief was slow to possess us, or, perhaps it possessed us so completely that none of us was able to devise a proper response.

"Look at Dad's hair," Auntie said to me.

Granddaddy presented a comical appearance. Part of his hair stood straight up on the top of his head. The rest of it clung tightly to his skull. Auntie laughed, and I laughed. Although there was a mirror a few steps away, Granddaddy stood where he was as if oblivious to our laughter.

What happened next is vague in my memory. I took Granddaddy back to my Armstrong grandparents' house, awakening my mother and her mother, who fixed breakfast for Granddaddy. They must have made breakfast for me as well and perhaps for themselves, but I can recall only that Granddaddy seemed to enjoy his bacon and eggs and drank a second cup of coffee. Auntie was alone with Chigger's corpse at the house on Shelby Avenue. She must have called the undertaker. I must have taken her to a telephone, but I cannot remember doing so or imagine now where, at three or four in the morning, a telephone could have been found. I do not recall much about Chigger's funeral. My mother told me to buy a white shirt, which I did, and I must have worn the shirt to the funeral that was held at the funeral home. But I do not remember the funeral. I do not remember looking at Chigger in her casket or riding to that familiar plot in Mount Olivet Cemetery. I do remember the grave. At Auntie's request, I took pictures of it, but the flowers that covered it were deprived of their beauty by the black-and-white film.

Auntie went to live with friends. Granddaddy and another old man took a small house in the country, "baching it," Granddaddy said, but after a month or two Auntie got a job as a waitress. She had never worked before, and being a waitress was probably the only job for which she was qualified. She could read and write, but her judgment was poor. Her mental capacity was never measured, but her IQ would have been low. Granddaddy was now seventy, too old to work, had work been available to him. But he had begun to get a small monthly stipend from the federal government, "old age assistance." With this and Auntie's pay and tips, they could live in reasonable comfort. Auntie was gregarious. The people with whom she worked, regular customers whom she served, became her friends. Granddaddy, home alone while she was working, sat on the porch or beside the fire and smoked his pipe. He was not a reader. He listened to the radio. Perhaps he replayed in his mind the stories that he had shaped by telling them often, but he no longer told them to me.

Auntie and Granddaddy remained in their small house in West Nashville for several years. They were there during the time I was in the Marine Corps. Finally, Granddaddy became too feeble to care for himself when Auntie was at work, and Auntie moved him to a nursing home that was run by the Little Sisters of the Poor. There was irony in this. Granddaddy had never been kindly disposed toward Catholics. He had criticized them for their vestments, their incense, their bells. In the short time that he lived in the nursing home, his friendly nature prevailed. The loneliness that he must have endured when Auntie was at work was relieved now. He had other old men with whom to talk, and he was good at that. In the summer of 1949, when Jane and I were just back from Iowa, he had a stroke, and a week or two later he died.

I do not know how Auntie felt about his death. She loved him. She took care of him as long as she could. But he was almost eighty years old, and Auntie must have had a sense of relief at his going. She had cared for him and Chigger for a long time. She was deeply weary. Like Chigger's, his funeral was in the funeral home, but unlike hers, his was conducted by the Reverend Florence Sullivan, for whom my father had been named before he changed the Florence to Laurence. It was an embarrassing funeral. Granddaddy's cousin Florence had scant skills as a public speaker. His theology was flawed beyond that of most Evangelicals, and he brought with him from his church a quartet that sang "The Old Rugged Cross" a cappella and in dubious harmony. But this part soon ended. We gathered at the cemetery under a blue sky and a few bright clouds. It was August, and the worst of the summer heat had receded. The day was perfect for a burial, at least for those of us who lived on.

Auntie soon got a job at the bus station restaurant, and she took a room within walking distance of her job. Periodically we talked on the telephone. I brought her to our house on Christmas Eve. I occasionally drove her to the cemetery, where we would linger a while around the familiar graves. She was not in good health. When she was sick, which was often, she would call me, and I would take her to the doctor or get her medicine from the drugstore or sit with her in her hospital room. She went once or twice to the City Hospital where Chigger and Grand-daddy had gone, but she had health insurance now. She had her own doctor, and she went as a private patient. Sometimes my mother and I helped her by paying part of her medical bills.

In 1964 Auntie went to Baptist Hospital for surgery to repair ad-hesions from an earlier procedure. For a while she seemed to be recov-ering. Then her wound festered and broke. She had peritonitis, the con-dition that had killed my father, but with antibiotics that began to heal. I went to see her every day, and since her infection was not fully cured, visitors, as well as nurses and doctors, wore masks and gloves and gowns in her room. She was able to get out of bed. One afternoon I found her sitting in a chair, an attendant brushing her hair. She seemed to be completely happy to have somebody care for her as she had spent her life caring for others. The next Sunday I was sick. I had a severe stomach-ache, perhaps contracted from her infection. I lay in bed most of the day in almost constant pain; but, late in the afternoon when the light was fading, the pain in my stomach stopped, and I could hear piano music—a recording? the radio?—from downstairs. I didn't recognize the music, which I thought was the saddest I had ever heard, but I hadn't enough energy to go downstairs and make the music stop. Outside the windows the darkness gathered. The music went sadly on, and my sor-row, which had no source or any meaning beyond itself, deepened. Auntie was dying, or would die within a few hours. I wondered later whether she might have felt that I had abandoned her. I hadn't called her to say that I was sick. She had been expecting me, and I had not come.

Auntie had the best of the Sullivan funerals. Hers, like those of her parents, was held in the funeral home; but Jane and I were still Episcopalians, and the associate rector at St. George's Church conducted the service according to the 1928 Book of Common Prayer. Soon we were back at Mount Olivet at the Sullivan plot, which I no longer visited except to take Auntie to decorate the graves. Her pallbearers were bus drivers, friends she had made when she worked at the bus station restaurant. They did their job, and soon Auntie was buried next to her mother and father as Granddaddy had planned. Jane and I and my mother and her husband stayed until the grave was filled, the dirt rounded, the flowers arranged on top of the bare earth. More than thirty-five years had passed since Granddaddy, Chigger, Auntie, my mother, and I had made our weekly pilgrimages to the place where my father's body lay. The trees had grown. The bench where we used to sit had long since rusted and been taken away. Many who had been alive when I was a child were no longer living. Not only Chigger and Granddaddy and Auntie but also "Titsy" Carter had died. My mother was sure, and I think she hoped, that he had had a third or fourth wife who had survived him. My mother's husband, who was already sick with cancer, would soon occupy the place that had been meant for me. In a few years my mother would occupy her place beside my father.

Chapter Two

Sturm und Drang

After my father's death, my mother and I lived with her parents on East Douglas Avenue. In my earliest recollections, the house was crowded. According to a newspaper account of their wedding, after their honeymoon my mother and father lived with Puver and Popoo, my Armstrong grandparents, until, I suppose, they could save or borrow enough to buy a house of their own. My mother's younger siblings followed her example. Her sister, my Aunt B—who was christened Willie B, but never went by the name of Willie—occupied one of the Douglas Avenue bedrooms with her husband, Herbert Slack. My Uncle Jim and his wife, Margaret, lived in another bedroom, which left one for my mother and me to share. Downstairs were a living room, a dining room, a kitchen, and a bedroom where Puver and Popoo slept. A room separated from the living room by French doors was called the sun parlor, but it did not seem to me to be any more sunny than the rest of the house. There was only one bathroom, which must have been much in demand, particularly in the morning, because, except for Puver and me, everyone in the house worked.

Popoo and B worked for the Louisville and Nashville Railroad. Herbert

Slack, who listened to grand opera on the radio and who had been a marine, owned a small printing business. Later he and B would divorce, and she would remarry. Jim was in charge of personnel at the Nashville Bridge Company. Margaret kept books at a Nashville department store. My mother taught at Lockeland School, and when the time came I was enrolled in nearby Eastland School, against my will, if not my better judgment. We had dinner every night at the round dining room table, which at mealtime was covered with a white tablecloth. This was before the Depression, before B's marriage began to collapse; and although I know now that she missed my father, my mother seemed to be one of a merry group that had no misgivings about the future. We ate the food that Puver cooked; we laughed, at what I do not know, but I remember that I laughed too, that somehow I was made a part of the adult conversation.

Jim and Margaret left first. They bought a house several miles out Gallatin Pike, on Winding Way, where they lived until they moved to a retirement home. B and Herbert stayed longer. When the economy got bad, Herbert moved his printing equipment from downtown to cramped quarters in a storeroom that had been built on the back of the house on Douglas Avenue—a blow to me because often Herbert had taken me with him when he returned to his shop at night. He had given me colored paper and pencils and buttons left over from old elections. Herbert's mind was filled with outlandish metaphors. He told me once that when you were fired from a job, someone stuck a fork in your nose. I believed him. When businesses began to collapse and people lost their jobs, I saw them in my imagination not only as poor but also with forks embedded in their noses. But then the Depression deepened and first B and then Popoo were dismissed from the railroad.

Everywhere, times were bad, but this was more than I could comprehend: too young to realize what was happening to my Sullivan relatives, I judged the world by the diminished fortunes of my family and my neighbors. My mother kept her teaching job, but her wages were decreased, and once or twice she was paid in scrip, a substitute for money that the government declared to be legal tender. Printed on colored paper, it looked phony, and nobody trusted it to retain its value. Jim was able to keep his house and his job, but he was scarcely able to make ends meet. One afternoon, in the living room, I saw Popoo give Jim a ten-dollar bill, and the look of sorrow and shame on Jim's face was etched in my memory. He was a grown man, but, incredibly to me then, he appeared to be on the verge of tears.

Popoo was rehired by the railroad because of the influence of Uncle Ben. Popoo's sister, Louella, had married Ben Heikens, a stern man of German descent who had a gift for getting ahead. He owned several farms near Decherd, Tennessee. Once when my mother and Puver and I were visiting him and Aunt Louella and he had taken me with him to feed some hogs, he told me that anyone who couldn't make a farm pay for itself in three years was "no farmer." Uncle Ben was a potato broker as well as a farmer. He had a potato house on a railroad spur where he graded and sacked and from which he shipped carloads of potatoes. A significant client of the railroad, he persuaded the railroad executives to put Popoo back to work. The railroad rehired Popoo but not at his old job. He became a night watchman at the L&N freight house.

Not long after he had to close his shop in town, Herbert moved his equipment out of the storeroom and was gone for good. That left five of us in the house where eight had lived, and soon, after a diligent courtship, B was gone too. She married Clem McDaniel, who in better days had sold paper to Herbert. They too bought a house off Gallatin Pike, but a year or so after B had moved out the Corder family moved in. My mother's older sister, my Aunt Janie, her husband, Walter Corder, and their daughters, Jeanette and Mildred, both slightly older than I, had once lived two blocks away from Popoo's house on Douglas. They had moved to Spartanburg, South Carolina, where a third daughter, Margaret, was born and where Uncle Walter had worked in an automobile dealership. He had an accident that destroyed an automobile, and he lost his position. This was not the first job he had lost, and it was not to be the last. To me his case was puzzling. He seemed to be a deeply confident man, happily sure of the validity of his own judgments, which, as psychologists have taught us to surmise, might have been his way of compensating to himself for his utter fecklessness. With the help of his sister's husband, who was secretary of the Nashville Chamber of Commerce, and sometimes that of Uncle Jim, Uncle Walter got job after job, advised his superiors how to run whatever business they were in, and soon was looking for a new situation. Almost every night at dinner during his periods of employment, he would repeat, with appar-

ent pride, the advice he had given his supervisor concerning how to
make the business go better. Even I knew that giving advice to those
who had authority over you was risky. My mother, who had heard Uncle
Walter brag too often to be surprised, was still astonished that he made
no connection between his own conduct and his series of short careers.
Most astonishing of all, Aunt Janie and the older girls congratulated
him on his wisdom. They were sincerely proud of his behavior. They
were convinced that, when he lost a job, he had suffered an injustice.

The Corders were still in Spartanburg when the East Nashville tornado destroyed our neighborhood. The storm came at the end of a day
that had been too warm, too still, too oppressive. I remember looking
out a window at the trees that were just beginning to bud, at the grass
that was turning green, at the buttercups, as we called them then, already
in blossom. There was no stir of air. Nothing moved. The world was so
absolutely still that peering through the window was like looking at a
painting. The boys with whom I ordinarily played were missing from
the sidewalk. Like my friends in other houses, like anyone who had
someone to hear his complaint, I criticized the weather. When my mother
came home from her school, she seemed more weary than usual.
Popoo, who slept in the daytime, had been restless and got up before
his accustomed hour. Twilight brought no relief. We had dinner, and
then, as she often did, my mother drove Popoo to the freight house,
and Puver and I went with them.
I liked to go to the freight house, where everything was different
from the things at home. There were desks and typewriters covered
against the dust and an enormous bottle of water turned upside down
with a spigot at the bottom and paper cups that were used once and
thrown away. Sometimes I went with Popoo into the cavernous shed
where the freight was stored and the darkness was barely penetrated by
the yellow light of Popoo's lantern. Even with Popoo holding my hand,
I was frightened. Where the light of the lantern did reach, it cast weird,
amorphous shadows; as we walked, the corner of a box, the slats of a
crate would appear suddenly out of the threatening darkness. There
were noises, too, real and imaginary. Rats scampered away from us;
boxes popped and creaked; I could always make myself believe that I
heard voices. I think now that Popoo was frightened too, an idea that

would have been utterly incredible to me seventy years ago. He was grown; he was big; he smoked cigars; he carried the lantern. When I expressed my fears, he said, "Don't worry, Mike, nothing's going to get you," using the name he had called my father and now passed down to me. But his voice was too loud. He was speaking not only to me but to anyone who might be lurking in our path. Now, I wonder if he talked when he was alone, not to himself, but to a make-believe companion.

On the way home that night, my mother stopped at a drugstore on Woodland street where I wanted to buy bubblegum. I was in the store when the storm hit. There was the usual roaring sound that people compare to a freight train, but a train is not quite what it sounds like. It's wind, and you know it's wind, but it is louder, the sound deeper, than any wind you have ever heard before. The sound seems to engulf everything, the air, the ground, the trees, the buildings. The sign that hung outside the drugstore swung up and blew away. Strange objects flew through the air: tree limbs, broken poles and planks, fragments of furniture, cushions, strips of paper, detritus too fragmented and moving too fast for me to identify. Rain came and obscured the outside world. The plateglass windows bowed in. Water came in around them and around the doors. The lights went out. I was more frightened than I had been with Popoo on his rounds. I wanted to get back to my mother, back to Puver. I started to leave the store, but a man caught me by the shoulder.

"Wait a minute, son," he said. "You can't go out in that."

The windows continued to rattle. The wind continued to roar. As the storm began to pass, we heard sounds of breaking glass and splintering wood and unknown things crashing together. Then the storm passed, and there was a moment of silence before the men who had been in the drugstore started talking all at once. The man who had been holding me released my shoulder. I went out onto the darkened sidewalk. At first, I didn't see my mother's car. Then I did see it, fifty feet down the street where the wind had carried it. I ran to it and got in with my mother and Puver, who, through the storm, had feared more for me than for themselves.

We started home, went a short way on Gallatin Pike, and were stopped by downed trees that blocked the road and downed electric wires that danced and sparked on the wet pavement. A few men, some of them with flashlights, arrived, kept their distance from the wires, and looked at the damage. Soon one of them came to tell my mother what we already knew: our way was blocked; nobody could guess when the road might be opened. We began to search for another way home, but we couldn't find one. We needed to go north, so we went over a block and found once more the fallen trees, the sparking wires, the men standing in the rain, pointing their flashlights. Here another man advised my mother that she and Puver and I should stay in the car. Our tires would protect us from the live wires that surrounded us, which may or may not have been true, but we took comfort in believing him. We went east and then west, and everywhere we were blocked. We could go back to town, and we did. We drove to the freight house, got Popoo, who left his job, and set out once more to find a way to our house if, as the adults wondered aloud, our house was still standing.

We drove across the Cumberland River, turned north on Dickerson Pike, went to Goodlettsville, then across to Gallatin Pike, far north of East Douglas Avenue. We saw no damage. There were lights in a few houses. But, when we went south again, the world was dark. I was worried. I knew that if our house had been blown away, we would have to look for a place to spend the night, and then look for a place to live. My mother and Puver and Popoo were thinking this too, and occasionally said so, but they were also wondering where they would get money to build another house if ours had been destroyed. So we rode, searching ahead of us for fallen poles and trees, driving slowly in spite of our anxiety. We passed familiar landmarks: the street where Jim and Margaret lived; the Methodist church where my mother sometimes took me on Sunday; we went down Shelton Avenue where the house that my mother owned stood intact. Our way was open, but increasingly we saw damage as we drove south: the same pattern of splintered trees; a bicycle lying on the street, a child's wagon overturned in the gutter. Now we rode in silence, too deeply concerned to articulate our fears. At last we moved up a darkened Douglas Avenue. The street was filled with trash, but the houses remained, as did ours.

I was greatly relieved, as I know the others were, but strangely we did not at first get out of the automobile. We waited for a moment without speaking. Then we did get out and went to the porch, where all the furniture was overturned and some of it was broken. Popoo retrieved the swing from the front yard and hooked it back on its chains. I helped him—or thought I was helping him—right the chairs, and we all sat down, still in silence.

"Well, thank God," Popoo said at last.

My mother and Puver murmured words of agreement.

As usual, the front door was not locked. My mother offered to take my hand, but this was not the freight house, and I wasn't frightened. Puver found a candle. By its frail light we walked through the house, but we found nothing wrong: no broken windows, no water on the floors, only the house as we had left it, but without electricity. I was very tired. My mother went with me upstairs, but I didn't need her. For this night, my fear had ended. I went quickly to sleep and slept until a morning that was bright and cool. I was delighted to learn that the schools were closed. I hurried through my breakfast and went out to join my playmates. We walked along the familiar streets and saw what everybody sees after a storm: denuded trees, poles without wires, tree trunks with pieces of splintered wood driven through them. Much was out of place. Freestanding woodsheds and workshops had been lifted out of yards and lay shattered on the pavement; some buildings had been turned to rubble.

The tornado had established its own path. The middle of a large three-story school was obliterated, its two ends left standing. At one house siding had been ripped off, but the studs and laths remained. At another the whole wall was gone, but inside the room pictures still hung on the walls, chairs remained upright, a lamp with its shade intact stood on a table. Unaccustomed objects were scattered across yards: books made worthless by the rain, a man's shirt, some dresses torn and spoiled by the mud, cooking vessels, a toy truck, a doll with a cracked head whose eyes remained open. A few of us tried to collect souvenirs, but whatever we took home our parents made us take back and leave at the place where we had found it. Nothing that was left by the storm belonged to us, and, however badly damaged it was, the owner still might use it. The storm had made bad times worse, particularly for those who had lost their property.

Late one afternoon, ten days or more after the storm, our lights came on. Upstairs and downstairs, all at once, the whole house was illuminated. A cheer went through the neighborhood. People went outside to congratulate each other. The next day our schools opened, but except for a few of the girls who always did as they were told and always made good grades, none of us felt like studying. Thoughts of the destruction we had seen, almost all of which still surrounded us, the memory of the storm through which we had lived, possessed our minds and tainted our behavior. We fidgeted at our desks; we broke line in the lunchroom; we fought each other on the playground. It took our principal, Mr. Sweeney, several days and several spankings to reestablish order.

Unlike Granddaddy, Popoo was not a gifted raconteur. Often he told us that he had driven his horse and buggy through a snowstorm on a past St. Patrick's Day, but the story had little detail and no dialogue. It was less a narrative than an admonition to those who tried to rush spring, and he told it every year to anyone who would listen. He raised chickens in his backyard, and for a while he raised pigeons. He undertook many projects. He built fences, built a stone wall in front of our house, planted trees and gardens. Before he retired from his night watchman's job, he prepared a surprise for the family. The makers of Hadacol, a patent medicine widely used in the 1930s, printed in the newspapers testimonials from and pictures of their satisfied customers. The morning that Popoo's picture and endorsement appeared in the *Tennessean,* he came into the kitchen where my mother and I were eating breakfast and Puver was drinking coffee, trying to suppress the smile that lifted the corners of his mouth, his eyes glowing with satisfaction. He placed the newspaper, opened to show his picture, on the table.

For a moment there was silence. Puver, who was not a demonstrative woman, who, most of the time, did not let her feelings show, was the first to speak

"Hadacol!" she said, her voice both outraged and angry. "You let them print your picture to sell Hadacol?"

At first, he was too pleased with himself to notice Puver's anger. "Yes," he said, "they gave me a copy of the picture."

"Daddy," my mother said, "you've disgraced us! You've disgraced the whole family!"

"Hadacol!" Puver said again. "You had no business doing this."

The phone began to ring. B called, Jim called, not to talk to Popoo, but to have their disapproval conveyed to him. Popoo's patience was limited, and his temper was short. My mother and Puver continued to scold him, and his anger increased. After each telephone call he raised his voice, no longer trying to defend himself, but taking the offensive, which was his usual posture. He considered the whole family a confederation of dolts and deplored their tastes as they deplored his. He was right, he said, and he demanded that Puver fix his breakfast.

While the others argued, I read Popoo's testimonial. Hadacol, he said, had improved his digestion, given him abundant energy, relieved his constipation, and—when I read it I began to laugh—cured his insomnia. Now, Popoo testified, for the first time in years, he was getting a good night's sleep. Did he sleep in the freight house? I wondered aloud. Did he snooze in the office among the desks and the shrouded typewriters? The others did not share my merriment. After an astonished silence, my mother and Puver once more took up the theme of Popoo's transgression. Nothing they said mattered to me. My mind was fixed on comedy. I wanted to take the newspaper to school, but the idea that I would make such a request further outraged my mother. Consequently I had nothing to show to amuse my classmates, but, following Granddaddy's example as well as I was able, I made the best story I could out of Popoo's sleepless nights at the freight house. Behaving as disgracefully as Popoo, I described the morning's furor and invented some dialogue that seemed to me to enhance the story.

Puver was my surrogate mother, and I think that Popoo would have been my surrogate father if he had known how. He was irascible, but my mother, who had many arguments with him, thought that he was not as irascible as he seemed. In his relationships, he employed a kind of wit that never quite worked. Jim and my Uncle Leonard knew how to tease. They accused me of having girlfriends that I didn't have and told me that I couldn't be as tall as I looked, but I knew from the tones with which they spoke that their remarks were rooted in affection. When Popoo spoke, the tone was seldom right. Most of the time, what he intended to be jocular sounded like criticism. As he grew older and became deaf, his efforts to establish family camaraderie were increasingly misunderstood. None of his relatives knew how to deal with him, but until his deafness prevented him from engaging in conversation, he had friends in the neighborhood, and he gathered a small group of retired men who drank coffee together.

Popoo, born in Middle Tennessee, was the son of a Methodist preacher. One of his cousins was superintendent of schools in Tullahoma or Manchester. His sister Louella had married rich Uncle Ben, who saved Popoo from poverty during the Depression. Most of his relatives were successful. One of his forebears was a general in the American Revolution. I do not know why, late in the nineteenth century, he left Tennessee and went to Texas. Puver's Fambro family was distinguished. Her father was a doctor, and her grandfathers on both sides were large landowners in Georgia. In the 1850s her Fambro grandfather moved his family to Texas to put them out of the way of the Civil War. When the war began, he became a Confederate bureaucrat. His sons and nephews fought for the Confederacy. Puver's father, who had served as chief surgeon in Pemberton's army, received a parole after the fall of Vicksburg. The terms of his parole prevented his return to the Confederate Army, but, for him, the war did not end at Appomattox. When he discovered that the history books his daughters studied in school referred to the Confederacy as "the enemy," he enlisted the help of the county judge. Together they burned the offending volumes and wrote a new book that was kinder to the South. After the war, he remained in Texas, married, fathered nine girls, and from time to time, according to Puver, drank too much.

Popoo first married one of Puver's older sisters, Nancy, who bore one son, Obie. He had a career in the army and died, I think of tuberculosis, before I was born. After Nannie, as she was called, died, Popoo married Puver. My Aunt Janie was born in 1896. Although she would never admit it—she always claimed to be younger than she was—my mother was born in 1898, like her sister in Center, Texas. In 1900, my Aunt B was born in Nashville, where later Jim was born, and where Puver and Popoo stayed for the rest of their lives. If it is true that opposites attract, theirs should have been a marriage made in heaven. Popoo had opinions, most of them bad, about everything and announced them to whomever would listen. Puver kept her own counsel. Usually, when Popoo fumed, she made no reply. She listened to soap operas on the radio, played solitaire at the dining room table, and oversaw the keeping of the house, but not to my mother's or B's satisfaction.

"Mama doesn't care how dirty the house gets," my mother said, "as long as there's no clutter."

"Mama sweeps the dust under the rug," B said.

Both of these statements told a part of the truth, but both were exaggerations. Once I got my own room, I found the house and the way Puver kept it quite comfortable. She was concerned about cleanliness, but she took housework in stride as she took everything else. What wasn't done today could be done tomorrow and, if not tomorrow, the day after that. Everything got done sooner or later, which, for better or worse, seemed to me to be a sensible view of how the world and all therein should proceed. I grew up not thinking that procrastination was a virtue, but I placed it among the most venial of sins.

My mother and I continued to live with Puver and Popoo until I left for the Marines in 1943. By then I had watched Popoo die. He had been ailing for months, but in that day there were no scans or sophisticated diagnostic tests, and few people went to a doctor for regular physical examinations. Years later, my mother failed in the same way Popoo had, and her symptoms were so much like his that I assumed, had he been properly diagnosed, that he, too, would have been found to have cancer of the pancreas. He had a sitter, maybe a licensed practical nurse, who stayed at his bedside at night as his death became increasingly imminent. The last few nights of his life, I slept on a couch in the sun parlor, and I was called in the depth of an early morning to stand with the sitter by his bed and watch him die. His death was similar to that of Chigger—the noise in his throat, the mucus on his chin, the irregular last breaths that he took. The sitter shut his eyes and pulled the sheet over his face. I went to awaken my mother.

I went to the Marine Corps a month after Popoo's death, and I never lived on East Douglas Avenue again. Not long after I got to Chapel Hill, my mother married William Burkhart. They moved to my mother's house on Shelton Avenue. After the war I lived with them until Jane and I married and went to Iowa, when I was twenty-three.

Chapter Three

Field and Stream

I think of my growing up, at least until I got to high school, as old-fashioned, with lots of boys for playmates and countless books filled with adventure to read, and no sense of any dangers lurking in the world beyond those that our minds could create. We had bicycles, and we were free to roam to Shelby Park and sometimes to Mr. Pickett's farm, which was on Neely's Bend Road near Madison. Mr. Pickett was our scoutmaster, a bachelor who lived with his parents in a spacious old house on what I now suppose was a small farm, but it seemed large to us, as well as almost inexhaustibly interesting. Unlike Uncle Ben's farms at Decherd, there was no pigpen here, but there were cows and a big garden and a large cornfield. Best of all, the Pickett farm bordered the Cumberland River, and there were flat-bottomed boats that we could take across the river. If we crossed the river early enough, we could see the sun rising behind the cornfield opposite the Pickett farm, and because it seemed an adventure to do so, we sometimes picked the corn across the river and tried, without much success, to roast it in a campfire. There was a house on the back of the Pickett farm, well separated from the residence, and we could stay there any time it wasn't occupied by one or another of Mr. Pickett's friends who, as I think we understood even then, took women there for romantic purposes. We learned to approach the cabin quietly; when somebody else was there, we built a fire and slept or, more likely, shivered through the night in a makeshift camp near the river.

Mr. Pickett was one of the toughest men I ever knew. He was small and wiry; I doubt that he weighed more than a hundred and fifty pounds. Whatever the weather, even the most frigid, he would take one of his boats out on the river wearing only his swimming trunks. He would stand in the back and guide and propel the boat by making the stern go up and down. I think he did this to set an example for his scouts because on these excursions he went nowhere in particular. He wanted us to know that he was tougher than we were. To the end of his long life he was proud of his physical achievements. I went to see him when he was well past eighty, rich from his dealings in real estate—he told me he owned thirty houses—and deaf as a post so that a conversation with him consisted principally of his telling stories I had heard before, but never tired of hearing. Besides playing football at Vanderbilt, he had sometimes joined a semipro team under an assumed name. He was what we called in those days a "ringer." His team went to Memphis to play an undefeated team sponsored by Clarence Saunders, "sole owner," as he liked to call himself, of a group of grocery stores in West Tennessee. Mr. Pickett was convinced that Saunders not only paid his players but also paid the officials. The first touchdown Mr. Pickett scored was canceled by a penalty. Again he scored, and again he was penalized. I think his third touchdown was called back too, but eventually the bribed officials had to let some scores stand, and Mr. Pickett's team was victorious. Mr. Pickett was also a boxer. He liked to tell of the fights he had had, and he very much liked to confirm that when you were hit hard, you did see stars, just as they drew it in the comic strips.

The river also ran beside Shelby Park, but the bank there was precipitous and cluttered with bottles and cans and paper plates, the detritus of picnics past and old drinking parties. I think a policeman was assigned to the park in the daytime, but we were more concerned with the people who ran the golf course. There was a free golf course at Shelby, but it was a sorry affair. The greens were cottonseed leveled and packed down. All the fairways ran straight from the tee to the green, and there was no rough to speak of. You could practice hitting a ball there, but not much else, so we tried, from time to time, to play a few holes on the real course without paying. We would start at the second or third hole, wherever we thought we couldn't be seen from the clubhouse, and we would play until an authority came in sight riding a tractor.

One morning I drove my ball straight and far down the fairway. I watched it hit and bounce and continue to roll, bright as a diamond against the short green grass. This was the best drive I'd ever made, perhaps the best drive that anyone had ever made, I told myself, and half believed it. I was so mesmerized by the beauty of my rolling ball that at first I was oblivious to the clanking sound of the tractor. When I did hear it, I feared that I had waited too long. My ball was lost and, with it, some of my pleasure. I would not get to stand where my ball had landed and look back in pride and wonderment at how far my ball had carried from the tee. My concern now was to escape. Holding my driver, I ran across the fairway and into the rough, up an incline that seemed steeper than it looked, trying to get to a patch of scrub trees before the tractor overtook me. My escape was a near thing. I was inspired by the sound of the tractor to run fast, faster than I had ever run before. I dared not risk slowing myself by looking back. I had only the sound of the tractor's rough engine to tell me how close I was to being captured, and, long before I got to the woods, I thought I was very close. I ran hard and breathed hard and, once I was sufficiently deep in the woods, I lay on the ground and panted, the air burning my lungs. Years later it occurred to me that my danger had not been as great as my imagination had made it. I doubt that little boys were sent to jail for not paying a greens fee.

At night the pursuing tractor had a light, easy to see from far away and easy to escape. After dark we waded in the pond on the course to retrieve golf balls. The water was filthy and the bottom was soft mud, but there was a constant supply of balls, most of them not very good because the golfers used their worst balls when they might be lost in the pond. We learned to lift the balls with our toes to avoid putting our faces in the water. We tried to be quiet so our presence would not be discovered, but usually, being young and exuberant, we failed. Pretty soon we would hear the tractor engine and see the tractor light moving down the fairway. It was easy then to leave the pond, grab our shoes, and escape to the dirt road where we had left our bicycles. We always escaped, but the darkness helped us to believe we were in danger.

Everything was new to us then, and it was easy, for me at least, to turn almost any experience into an adventure. There was a railroad trestle near the park that spanned a gulch too steep for trains or even pedestrians. I don't know how long the trestle was, but it seemed very long to us, and, sooner or later, all of us had to walk across it. There was a water barrel about halfway across where you could stand off the track if a train caught you in midpassage. Otherwise you had to beat the train to the other side of the trestle. Was this as dangerous as we thought it was? It appeared to us to be a long way across, and when we saw the trains pass, as we sometimes did, they seemed to be going very fast, certainly a lot faster then we could run on the crossties. Whoever was going to indulge this rite of passage would listen carefully for any sound that a train was coming. Then he would cross as fast as he could, and always he made it safely. Once you had crossed you had to come back. The gulch was impossible to navigate.

Three or four blocks from where my friends and I lived there was a hill with a substantial house on top of it. The property consisted of several acres with a paved drive that wound up to the house past a gasoline pump, the first privately owned pump any of us had ever seen. Although the house was vacant, the property was still maintained, the grass cut, the shrubs pruned, the trim occasionally painted. We were told, I don't remember by whom, that the man who had owned the house had killed himself, so for us the house had the aura of death. It was spooky. None of us went there alone, and we never went there at night even in one another's company. Even on the brightest days, we could not forget that the house was haunted because a man had died there. We followed the long driveway though sunlight, exchanging the stories that we always told when we made this journey. Each of us had heard a different version of the late owner's death. We agreed that he had killed himself. Whether true or not, this was an accepted fact in our neighborhood. But how? I clung to the theory—I still do—that he had shot himself. Johnny said he had hanged himself, but where had he attached the rope? From looking in the windows, as we always did, I could not see a place convenient for hanging. Henry thought a knife had been involved, but this was too bloody and violated my sense of the romantic aspect of whatever had happened here.

One Sunday afternoon we found an unlocked window and opened it. Then we stood and looked at each other waiting for somebody to volunteer to go in first. Nobody did. We drafted Henry because he was smallest and we could lift him up and shove him in. I got to go last because I had the longest legs, which should have made my entry easy because I would be among friends, but they had gone to another part of the house. I was alone in a room that was devoid of furniture. The walls seemed freshly painted. The floor was polished. There was nothing here to see, nothing to feel, since the ghost of the dead man had not come among us. Would he come? Would we feel his presence when we got to the room where he had committed suicide? It was easy for us to think so, easy for us to believe that the dark stain on one of the floors was the blood of the man who had taken his own life. I tried to see him lying there. I wondered if he had dropped his gun. Then I shivered with cold and fear, and at once we all ran for the open window. Henry got there first and was soon out. Johnny pushed me away and left. Last in, I was the last out. I was frightened, scared by my own imagination— or maybe something else. I was young. I put a good deal of faith in my instincts.

The other haunted house in our neighborhood was next door to Eastland School, and its backyard was a part of the school playground. The house was a two-story white brick much favored by pigeons who sat in a line along the ridgepole, no more frightened by the rumor of ghosts than they feared my friends and me, even though we occasionally shot at them with our BB guns. Unlike the house on the hill, no rumor of death was attached to the house next door to the school. Often the school janitor went in and out carrying tools or lumber or sacks of whatever he needed to take care of the school. Clearly the house was as innocent as our storeroom at home, much less forbidding than the freight house where every night Popoo walked among shadows. Most days after school we tried the doors, and one day we found one unlocked. We went into the musty rooms, which were filled with cans of old paint, discarded plumbing fixtures, a bucket, a broom, a mop. The floors were dirty, the fireplaces full of trash. The rooms upstairs looked the same, but nobody volunteered to go down into the unlighted basement.

That night we returned with our flashlights, and all was different. Except in the places where we pointed our lights, the rooms were dark but far from silent. The old house creaked and groaned. It snapped and popped. We had come into the house talking, teasing each other, claiming that we wouldn't be afraid to be in the house alone or to spend the night there if we had to. The noises that the house made silenced us. Suddenly, fear possessed us. One of us moved toward the door, and the others followed, pushing each other, stumbling, and cursing. Then we were outside, embarrassed at our display of cowardice, but not so much so that any of us went back into the house or went close enough to shut the door.

At the end of the fifth or sixth grade, I left Eastland and went to Bailey school, which had been completely restored since the tornado. At Bailey, for the first time, I had different teachers for different courses, and there was a large study hall where we stayed when we were not in class, with an unabridged dictionary that we could consult and in which we looked up words such as *bitch* or *bastard* or *whore;* seen in print, the words assumed a sterner reality. I saw pornography for the first time on the playground at Bailey. I never knew where they came from, but frequently a classmate would have one of the small books that circulated surreptitiously then, takeoffs of comic strip characters that were extremely vulgar. We had to read them fast, because when Mr. Sweeney, the principal who had come with us from Eastland, saw a group of boys looking at something, he came to see what we were looking at.

Mr. Sweeney gave me the only spanking I ever got in school. For reasons unfathomable, a boy brought a cardboard box to school, which was asking for trouble. The boy sitting in front of him in the study hall kicked the box up the long aisle toward the front of the room. Then Charlie, with whom I had had to swap verses in the fourth grade because he wouldn't say "U is for underwear," kicked the box, and then I kicked it. The first kicker escaped, but the study hall teacher, who, like a thousand other teachers you have heard of, was said to have eyes in the back of her head, sent Charlie and me to Mr. Sweeney. Mr. Sweeney told us to go to the men's room, and he followed with his paddle concealed under his coat. He told Charlie to stick out his hand, and Mr. Sweeney whopped it. I stuck out my hand and got my whop, then Mr. Sweeney whopped us again. This was painful, but I don't think Mr. Sweeney was hitting me as hard as he was hitting Charlie, who, in spite of his reluctance to discuss undergarments in public, was a more notorious misbehaver than I. When Mr. Sweeney set out to give us our third whop, Charlie tried to avoid putting his hand out. "Give me that hand!" Mr. Sweeney commanded. Charlie did, and we got more whops before Mr. Sweeney dismissed us. Charlie was crying, which is another reason that I think he got hit harder than I did. He shouldn't have been crying. We were in the eighth grade. We were too old to cry. The next year we would be going to East Junior High, a large school on a large campus in a more interesting part of town.

There was plenty of space on the East High campus for walking and playing and misbehaving if you were so inclined. There were two main methods of misbehavior. One was smoking, which I had not yet begun, and the other was leaving the campus during school hours, which I did frequently. Often, usually with friends, I would go to Brown's Drug Store, which was a block down and across the street from school property. The store was owned by J.P., who was the older brother of one of my classmates. Although he became successful later, J.P. was deeply in debt, having recently bought the store. He seemed always to be working, and I think he put up with us reading his magazines and loafing around his premises in exchange for the sporadic business we gave his soda fountain, the nickels we dropped in his pinball machine, and, later, the loose cigarettes we bought for a penny each. One day, I was at J.P.'s with two companions—neither of them the notorious Charlie—when the crossing guard took us into custody. The guard's name was Braxton Duke. He was on his way to a career in the police force in which he rose to high rank, and I did not doubt his authority to take us to Mr. Lipscomb, the principal of East Junior. Duke, as all the students called him, ordered us to come with him, and he led us out of the store and turned left toward the school. I had put myself last in our line of march. When Duke went left, I turned right. In two steps, I was around the corner of the drugstore and running across the parking lot of the ice cream parlor next door. I hid for a while in a garage, then took a careful and circuitous route back to the campus. Duke, surer of himself than he had a right to be, didn't discover my absence until he and his other captives reached the school.

"Where is the boy in the green hat?" he wanted to know. This was an accurate description. I did have a green hat that I wore almost everywhere.

My companions could answer truthfully that they did not know. "What's his name?" Duke asked.

Less truthfully, they claimed not to know that either.

Mr. Lipscomb punished both of the miscreants. They had to lean over and get swatted with a paddle bigger than the one Mr. Sweeney used on hands. They said this was a painful experience, and they had their revenge on me for having missed it. A day or two later, when school was out and we were crossing Gallatin Pike, they began to yell at Duke. "Hey, Duke!" they said. "Hey, Duke! Here's the boy in the green hat."

It was true. I was still wearing my hat, and I escaped because Duke couldn't stop directing traffic to chase me. At first it seemed to me that I faced a dilemma. I could stop crossing Gallatin Pike where most of my friends crossed and where Duke directed traffic. Or I could abandon my hat. Then I saw that I now had a real adversary. I was no longer running from ghosts or from trains that kept roughly to their schedules. My hat was my symbol of victory as long as I could keep wearing it, as long I didn't get caught by Duke.

When I enrolled in East Junior High School, I had been playing the trumpet in the school band for several years; now I had my first experience with a group that played popular music. Mark, a Vanderbilt student who was very bright and a fine musician, organized what we hopefully called a swing band. Using stock arrangements, we began to rehearse. I never fully understood why Mark wanted to fool with us. He played clarinet and alto and tenor sax, and he was so good that, in my judgment, he could have played with almost anybody who needed a reed player. Maybe he simply liked to be the leader, but for whatever reason, he taught us a lot, and we must have annoyed him grievously with our incompetence. Mark lived with his family on Eastland Avenue in a house nicer and more spacious than the houses in which most of us lived, and our band rehearsed in his living room. Mark's poor parents retreated to their bedroom upstairs, but they must have been sorely tried by our loud efforts to make music. Gradually, we became sufficiently competent to play for school assemblies, and, now and then, we got a small job playing for a dance or at a nightclub. We mostly played for fun.

Mark graduated from college and went somewhere—maybe to the army, because by now, in 1939, the war had begun in Europe and men were being drafted for military service in the United State. A classmate of mine organized a band that consisted mostly of musicians, if you could call us that, from Mark's old organization. Until now we had known our new leader as Clarence Dick, but he now claimed that his middle name was Sylvester, and he billed himself as Syl Dick, which wasn't bad in any discernible way but still seemed to suggest something off-color. Syl's mother—we were all willing to accommodate his new name— seemed to be moderately affluent. As the band was getting organized, she paid us fifty cents each for all rehearsals. We took up where Mark's band had left off, playing at school gatherings and at a few paying jobs, but it was hard for the band to maintain continuity. Some of the members of the group graduated from high school. They could be replaced, but not with the ease with which real professionals could step into a job, read whatever music was set before them, and discern the style of the band, however it differed from that of others. We broke up into little groups that played occasionally in roadhouses for not much money.

Chapter Four

Innocence Lost

The winter of 1940–1941 was so bitterly and unrelentingly cold that, to the astonishment of the sensible and the delight of the foolhardy, the Cumberland River froze. Nashville folklore claimed that the river had frozen a hundred and fifty years before when settlers had first come from North Carolina and Virginia, but nobody alive in 1940 had seen it frozen, and it has not frozen since. Some of us walked across it, slipping and sliding and sometimes falling down, oblivious to the fact that if the ice broke we would be swept away by the current and drowned. One man drove across the ice in an A-model Ford and got his name and his picture in the newspaper. The rest of us were content with being able to say that we had walked across, and probably venturing out on the ice was less dangerous than some of the things my friends and I had done in our youth: walking across the railroad trestle, speeding blindly up and down hills so steep that they blocked the view in front of us. The river remained frozen for a week or so, and even long after the ice had melted, the water stayed cold.

One day in April, Tommy, my best friend in high school, and I skipped our classes and took to the river in a borrowed canoe that we soon capsized, dumping ourselves into frigid water. I was not a strong swimmer, and I suggested that we stay with the canoe and push it toward the shore, but Tommy said no, so we struck out for the riverbank, which seemed to me to be too far away for us to reach.

"You can make it," Tommy said. "You've got to."

I swam the backstroke, with which I made a slow progress, but the backstroke seemed less tiring to me than any other. It was also better not to see the shore, not to know how much farther I had to go and be discouraged. The water seemed to get colder as I swam, which it didn't, of course, but I did. My muscles ached and I was out of breath. Finally I was sincerely afraid that I wouldn't get to the bank, that I would drown, which some people always did in the spring when the water was most treacherous. When I was convinced that I couldn't swim any farther, Tommy grabbed me by the hair and pulled me ashore. We borrowed a boat and rescued the canoe, but, to the canoe owner's chagrin and ours too, we did not find the paddle.

Then it was summer and hot, and I got a job at the Nashville Bridge Company, where I had gone years before with my Uncle Jim when the river had flooded and the shop and the giant machines it housed were half submerged. I was a layout man's helper, and Doc, the layout man I helped, worked diligently to keep from working. We were building mine-sweepers to send to England under the Lend-Lease program. Doc read the blueprints and drew in chalk on large steel plates the shapes of smaller plates that would be a part of the ship's hull. With a hammer and a punch, I made indentations on the plate, leaving a dotted line to guide the man who cut the plates if, as usually happened, the chalk lines were obliterated. This was not a bad job, but Doc wouldn't let me do it. He would draw a plate or two, and I would make my dots. Then he would lead me into the hull of one of the unfinished minesweepers. The hulls where we hid were open above where the deck would later be, but there were no portholes, no cross breezes, and heat shimmered off the plates made hot by the sunshine. Doc smoked a cigarette, against the rules for us during working hours. We sat on upturned kegs or boxes or, sometimes, narrow metal ledges the welders had left, but this was the hottest place of all, and I tried not to sit there. Our sweat dripped. Smoke from Doc's cigarette languished in the motionless air. All around us, work went on, and the noise of it—the banging of hammers, the rapid blows of air chisels chipping off spots of careless welds—echoed sharply from one side of the hull to the other. Occasionally I remembered how cold the river had been when Tommy and I fell into it in April, but memory had no force against the heat.

How Doc's working life played out, I don't know, but I was soon transferred to the "bull gang." This was a job that almost nobody wanted. The shop covered several acres, and steel had to be moved from one place to another. After the plates that Doc laid out had been cut, they went to the "hot floor," where they were bent to fit the ship. Then they were taken to the ships, mostly an easy passage since the land sloped downward toward the river. Without any exception that I can remember, all the steel was moved by human effort. Some went on carts that ran along rails, pushed from one place to another by members of the bull gang. Beams—we were still building bridges as well as ships—and heavy plates were lifted by cranes that ran on tracks just under the roof. These were also pushed, and they were hard to move and dangerous. Although nobody put it in these terms, I was soon made to understand by my fellow workers that anything that could be lifted could fall. Any part of your body that was under what fell would be obliterated. I was given rough, often profane, instructions by men I had only recently met to keep my body out from under beams and plates until staying clear of lifted steel became a habit.

Almost everybody in the bull gang had a nickname. Mine was Popsicle—which I didn't particularly like—but which I was given because I reminded the men with whom I worked of a previous member of the bull gang who had been called Popsicle. I didn't have the courage to ask whether the first Popsicle had been a good worker. I answered when I was spoken to and got used to what I was called. Unlike mine, most nicknames, in the bull gang as elsewhere, were descriptive. Men were named for the color of their hair or for other physical characteristics: Red, Cotton, Blackie, Baldy; Shorty, Fats, Slats, Slim, Skinny. To our more sensitive ears, many of the nicknames used in those days sound cruel. People with speech impediments were sometimes called "Dummy." If you talked too much you were called "Windy." The foreman of the bull gang walked with a limp and was called Crip. Crip was admirable in his simplicity. He lived on Shelby Avenue, a mile or so from the Bridge Company, and, despite the catch in his stride, he walked to and from work.

On Mondays when others, occasionally including Doc, arrived with bru-
tal hangovers or faces scarred from fighting or eyes cast down by feelings
of guilt over squandered paychecks, Crip came wearing clean, pressed
overalls, his round face innocent and unlined, although he was in his
fifties. He found hard jobs for me, not because he wanted to punish me,
but because he thought, rightly, that my body needed to be strength-
ened. Working made the time pass. I was often surprised when the
whistle signaled that it was time for lunch or that the day had ended.

Early in the summer I heard of an English-made Austin automobile
for sale for fifteen dollars. The black paint on the Austin was dull and
in spots worn through; the tires were bald; the windshield had been
replaced by a piece of plate glass that did not quite fit and rattled along
with other parts of the car that I could not identify. The Austin had no
key. There was simply a switch to be turned, and I got in the car and
turned it and pressed the starter. The engine caught less reluctantly
than I would have predicted. I put the car in gear, I released the clutch,
and the Austin made a slow but distinct progress up and down the lot.
In a transaction primitive by today's protocols, I paid the fifteen dollars
in cash, one dollar more than my weekly pay at the Bridge Company,
and I drove the first automobile I ever owned south on Gallatin Pike to
Douglas Avenue.

The Austin required considerable attention. It used oil as if that was
its fuel. I asked for and got, from a nearby filling station, old oil that
had been drained from newer crankcases. Keeping the tires inflated was
more complicated. I had a pump, a jack, a lug wrench, a tire tool, a
patching kit. When a tire went flat, I examined the casing for nails; I
inflated the inner tube, submerged it in water to find the leak, then
patched it and put the tube and the tire and the rim of the wheel back
together again. This was easier than it sounds because the wheels, like
the rest of the automobile, were very small. I never knew what year the
Austin had been made, but, like most automobiles of the late twenties
and early thirties, it looked like a box or, rather, two boxes, one placed
lengthwise above the wheels, the second placed vertically on top of the
first. The front seat was narrow in both directions, a tight fit for two
people; there was no space behind it, and there was no trunk. The spare
tire was attached to the rear of the car. The space under the hood, though
far from commodious, was ample for the small engine.

I drove my Austin to work and drove it on weeknights to the drug-store or to the poolroom or to wherever my friends and I had agreed to congregate. On weekends I borrowed my mother's car or rode with others who had better cars than I. Often, on the weekends, we drove fifty miles over passable roads to Dunbar Cave, which was just over the Tennessee line in Kentucky. The stone surface at the mouth of the cave had been polished smooth. There were lights and a bandstand, and air from the cave cooled the dance floor. Often there was no band to play, but there was a jukebox that got a lot of use, sometimes even on Satur-day morning. J.P., who owned the drugstore where my friends and I often gathered, and Hazel, his wife, rented a house not far from the cave, and we often stayed there, the girls inside, the boys out. In clement weather the boys slept on the ground. If it rained, we tried to sleep on the porch, but the porch was harder than the ground, and neither place was conducive to sound sleeping. We would be awakened by the first morning light, or somebody would be, and he would wake the rest of us because that is the way boys treat each other. We would relieve ourselves behind a tree and wait for the girls to arise and prepare them-selves to meet the day, which took forever.

In the dining room of the rented house, J.P. dealt blackjack. He had more money than the rest of us, so he could cover all bets, and he knew that the odds of the game favored the dealer. When someone else won the deal, J.P. would buy it back—usually for a quarter or thirty-five cents because we played a nickel-and-dime game—and continue slowly but surely to take our money. When Jean, my girlfriend during most of my high school days, and I were at odds, I played a lot and in the long run lost what then was a lot of money. Above the table where we played, the air was gray with smoke. Music came continually from a record player, songs that Hazel liked, mostly slow ballads about unrequited love except for the Andrews Sisters singing of a springtime wedding. I watched my nickels and dimes disappear. I would have been better off financially if I had stopped arguing with Jean. The game never faltered. Boys and their dates walked on the Dunbar Cave grounds, swam in the pool, sat close to each other on the grass or on benches and longed for darkness, but there were always enough unattached males for the game to con-tinue. The girls, none of whom played, could cook at J.P.'s house, and they often gave us dinner. The boys kept themselves presentable by showering and shaving at the bathhouse at the pool, but some of us didn't require daily shaving. We had changes of underwear, but our shirts and pants had to last us for the weekend. The girls, free from their parents, lived according to relaxed rules of their own devising. They stayed out later than they did at home, but they all returned to J.P.'s at the same time, because, I suppose, they didn't want to be talked about.

My estrangement from Jean was a familiar part of our stormy relationship. In high school I had occasionally dated other girls, often when a boy was needed for a dance, but Jean was the only real girlfriend I had ever had. I do not remember the first time I went out with her. When I was in the tenth grade, fifteen years old and inexperienced and shy, I admired her from a distance. Like Scarlett O'Hara, she was not beautiful, but her face was strong and handsome with large eyes and a prominent nose and full lips. She had lots of clothes, skirts and blouses and sweaters that always fit well. I thought her legs were gorgeous. She seemed to be, and I think was, the most sophisticated of all the girls I knew. All girls didn't smoke then, but Jean did. She said "damn" and "hell," which were daring words for girls to use at that time. Later, she would have a drink, but she was a careful drinker. When we were seniors in high school, we were "going steady," as we used to call it, neither of us dating anybody else except for the times that we argued and separated. Conventional wisdom says that "opposites attract," but Jean and I were very much alike in temperament and disposition. We both had quick tempers; both of us were overly sensitive, ready to take offense at small incidents, things done or said that shouldn't have bothered us, and our stubbornness kept us from making up quickly. In our good times, we planned to marry, but, if we had, our marriage would have been a disaster. Long ago, when I recalled our Dunbar Cave days, I thought of our sleeping arrangements there as a rough image of our relationship: she in the house, I in the yard, neither of us fully comfortable.

My male friends and I happily continued our frivolous existence. Glenmore bourbon cost eighty cents a pint. When I was still in high school, four of us would contribute twenty cents each and sit in a parked car and talk and pass our bottle. Sometimes we would sing, our harmonies egregious even to our own prejudiced ears. Now and then, when we hit a proper chord, we would congratulate ourselves, but good or bad, or, I should say, bad or good, we enjoyed singing. Because we were all working and had more money than before we graduated, we took our bottles to Dunbar Cave, where the whiskey helped us sleep but was hardly conducive to prudence. At the urging of Tommy and Malcolm, a mechanical genius who had put an eight-cylinder engine and a frame to support it under the body of a T-model Ford, I agreed to drive my Austin to Dunbar Cave.

Malcolm had taught me how to keep my Austin running. He and Tommy promised to follow me and help me if their help was needed, but they gave me more help than I expected. With its accelerator fully open and its engine straining, my Austin would not quite go fifty miles an hour. Now Tommy and Malcolm—I don't remember which of them was driving—put their bumper against mine and pushed my car. The engine raced; the speedometer climbed. I managed to shift into neutral, which took the strain off my engine, but with my motor idling my headlights, none too bright under the best circumstances, dimmed. I could barely make out the road. I leaned forward and clung to the steering wheel. My car was moving faster than it had ever gone since I had owned it. I had seen the speedometer reach fifty, and I knew that we— Tommy and Malcolm and I—were still accelerating. I kept my eyes on the road, trying to see, trying not to miss a curve. I was concerned about my tires, worn thin, unreliable even at slow speeds. I cursed Tommy and Malcolm, an otiose waste of breath since they couldn't hear me, and nothing I said could assuage my fears or ameliorate my situation. I thought I was going to be killed, which made me as angry as I was scared. Then Tommy and Malcolm backed off in time for me to coast into a filling station.

"Sullivan," Tommy said, "let that be a lesson to you. Never drive a car any faster than it will go."

Malcolm's car always ran well, and Tommy had a reliable A-model Ford, but our most memorable trips to Dunbar Cave were made in vehicles that were likely to betray us. Randall, another friend and class-mate, briefly owned an automobile that was already antique in 1941. Was it a Packard? A Pierce-Arrow? A Cadillac? Probably it had come from some company long out of existence, but in its day it had been elegant. Whether it had been a convertible or simply had lost its top, I do not know, but it was open to the prevailing elements. Its paint, originally a dignified maroon, was scaling in places. The black leather upholstery

was scuffed and torn. But, like my grandfather's Dodge that I remembered from childhood, it had brackets that had once held bud vases
and a compartment for a picnic basket. It had a tool chest, now bereft
of tools, and two spare tires, one on each front fender. Its large wheels
with wooden spokes lifted it high off the pavement. But in spite of its
age and its stiff springs that conveyed to the passengers each shock of
the road, to romantic souls, just out of high school, it was luxurious.

Late one afternoon, and a weekday afternoon at that, Randall and I
and one or two friends set out in the old car for Dunbar Cave. We went
slowly through the late afternoon, the breeze made by the car's motion
gentle and pleasant. People stared at us as we passed, surprised to see
such an ancient vehicle. We chugged along, moving slowly up hills. Once
or twice, I wondered if we would have to get out and push or perhaps
put the car in reverse and back up the hills as we sometimes used to
have to do in T-models. No such thing was necessary. We drove well over
an hour to go fifty miles. We arrived at J.P.'s in the final fading light.
The girls and the few boys who were there on this weeknight gathered
around to look at our car, the girls flattering our male egos by telling us
how brave we were to come in the car all the way from Nashville, the
boys expressing disgruntled doubts and predicting, all too accurately,
that we would have trouble with the car before we got home again.
Jean and I were still sulking; breaking up was easier than making up for
both of us. Stubborn as we were, we each waited for the other to offer
some gesture. On this night Jean joined the group gathered around our
automobile. The gentle girls and the rude boys finished admiring or
condemning our car and moved back toward the house. Jean sat down
on the front steps, lit a cigarette, and looked off toward the darkness. I
hesitated. Then I went and sat down beside her and lit my own cigarette.
For a while, we smoked in silence.

"Well," I said finally, "how have you been?"

"Missing you," she replied, and we were back together again, to walk
the dimly lit paths, to sit on a bench in the darkness.

While we sat out of sight of our friends, we thought only of ourselves,
the dreams we had, the foolish plans we made for the future. It seems
strange to me now that we could have known as much as we did about
the fighting in France, the bombing of England, the preparations for war
that were being made in our own country and still think of ourselves as

separate from all of it. Or rather, not think, but simply drift along entranced by our own callow emotions. I read the newspapers that told of battles and of death and destruction, but like most of my contemporaries, in my imagination, war was still what I had seen in films, heroic action, the deaths of others, but never your own death, never the pain that might precede it. We dreamed our impossible dreams and remained separated in our minds from the world's reality.

But our old automobile was real enough, and we had to return to Nashville in it. My friends were ready to leave when I got back to the house with Jean. We waved good-bye to those who were still there and still up. Randall started the car, and away we went, making our slow way home, almost quiet because we were sleepy and knew we had far to go and would have to go to work the next morning. We drove for half an hour or so. Then without preamble—no sputters or misfires or loss of power—the engine stopped. Randall tried to start it, but it would not start. The feeble battery turned the starter more and more slowly. We needed Malcolm, but Malcolm was doubtless at home in bed, and even if we had had a way to call him, he likely didn't love us enough to come miles in the depth of the night to assist us. We tried to look at the engine, but in the darkness we could see nothing. We lit matches. We burned our cigarette lighters until the fuel gave out. We scorched our fingers trying to make the matches last.

"What's usually wrong?" I asked Randall because for my Austin I had a menu of recurring faults, a checklist in my head of things that often caused trouble.

"I don't know," Randall said. "I just got the car yesterday."

We saw that the fan belt was tight. There was water in the radiator. We jiggled the spark plug wires. We looked for anything we could push or pull or turn to tighten. When we had tampered with every part of the engine we could find, Randall got in the driver's seat and pressed the starter again, but again nothing happened. Our matches were gone; our lighters would no longer burn. We cursed for a while. Then in darkness we punched and pulled and jiggled what would jiggle. Suddenly, for reasons that none of us would even try to guess, the engine started.

We had a tense ride home. We listened to the engine, to strange noises that it made, each of which suggested that it might stop once more and never start again. Our slow pace, which had not bothered us on the trip up, made our passage seem interminable. We looked for familiar landmarks and found them, but they were long in coming. In Nashville, at last, we went to a filling station that we knew stayed open all night. It was owned by the father of one of our friends, and in a continuation of our bad luck, the person scheduled to work at night had not shown up; our friend's father was running the station. It was well after midnight. Those of us in the car were tired and unhappy. Doubtless our faces were dirty from the ride, and we smelled of whiskey. We had probably awakened our friend's father, who was not accustomed to working at night, but he was a gregarious man, and we had assuaged his loneliness. He looked at us dubiously. He greeted us by name. He asked us where we had been and what we had been doing, implying with the tenor of his questions, half friendly, half accusatory, that he knew that we had been misbehaving, but to show what an amiable man he was, he would keep what he knew to himself.

"We're having car trouble," Randall said.

"I should think so," our friend's father replied. He knew what make the car was and said so, but none of us cared by then. He claimed to know the model year, but whether he did or not didn't interest us. "Who owns this car?" he asked.

Randall confessed that he did and became the focus of the man's attention.

"Well," he said, "this is a very old car, and I'm sure it's not going to run much longer. You were foolish to drive it on the highway. You're lucky you got back."

This, we had to confess to ourselves, was all too true.

"Do you need oil?" the man asked, "do you need gas? I can sell you oil and gas, but, if you need anything else, I'm afraid I'll have to disappoint you."

We were ready to leave, longed to do so, but we had been taught to be respectful to adults, and our friend's father was fully awake and apparently meant to make the most of our company. He told us again the age of the car. He opened the hood, lifting both sides, for that is the way hoods opened on old cars, and pointed out that no part of the engine was familiar to him. He named the carburetor; the distributor, whether or not the old car had one; the spark plugs, in which he took some delight.

"Look at the plugs," he said. "I couldn't even replace those for you."

He examined the engine further, named other parts. He seemed to me to be overly joyful discussing the cause of our night's misfortune. He talked and we half listened. I longed to be in bed, to get a little sleep before I had to go to work, and home was still too far away for me to walk and hope to get there before breakfast.

"Obsolescence," our friend's father said, his voice firm and judicial. "That's the trouble with your car. Obsolescence."

Obsolescence was not a word any of us used, but we knew what it meant. It occurred to me that it could refer to our interlocutor too, for he was probably as old as the car, and, at this moment, he was equally aggravating. He was still talking when we cranked up and drove away, again moving slowly, again fearful that the car would betray us.

"Well," I said when Randall let me out at my house, "it's been a hell of a night."

Randall agreed, and we laughed quietly, happy to be home, happy to have survived our adventure, now that we had survived it.

I stood on the sidewalk and watched Randall leave, the red glow of his taillight growing small and dim and disappearing into the darkness. I lingered for a moment longer on the sidewalk. Then I went into the house and up the stairs to my room and lay down without undressing.

Chapter Five

Beginning Again

I entered Vanderbilt in late September 1941, slightly more than two months before the Japanese bombed Pearl Harbor. I would not be eighteen until January. Even for seventeen, I was immature and shy and deeply insecure, and I felt that I had been precipitated into an alien world where people were neither friendly nor hostile, but indifferent to my very existence. In a way, this was true. I don't know how many of those who graduated from East High when I did entered college, but, of those who did, no more than four or five went to Vanderbilt. Whatever the demographics actually were, it seemed to me that all the students were rich, that many of them had known one another before they came to Vanderbilt, and that they had scant interest in enlarging the circle of their acquaintance. I know now that this was not true. After the war, the ambience that had seemed so snobbish to me when I was a freshman I saw anew as very friendly. Being with my fellow students made my last year or so at Vanderbilt in 1946–1947 a time of great happiness.

However friendly or unfriendly my classmates of 1941 were, I was partially kept out of the main flow of campus life because I lived so far from the campus. Usually I came to the campus, met my classes, and went home. Actually I frequently didn't meet my classes, and now I can't possibly say why. Why did I not want to learn? Why did I not want to enter into the intellectual life of the college? It is painful to recall the opportunities I missed, the time I wasted. I enjoyed English, but Edwin Mims, who lectured to all freshmen one day a week, assigned many passages of poetry to be memorized, and I almost failed the first term of English because I didn't accomplish the memory work. My faculty adviser, assigned to me by the university, enrolled me in chemistry, which came very close to creating disaster. I didn't like the subject. I didn't like the laboratory work. Sometimes I skipped the weekly stint in the lab, and I was given an F for the work I hadn't done.

I think that one absence on my record was justified. I had mathematics, which I didn't like and in which I didn't do well under a professor who bragged that he had flunked Red Grange, a legendary football player, when he was teaching math at the University of Illinois. I suppose he meant by this that if he had flunked Grange, he would not hesitate to flunk us, and I believed him. My math class on Monday, December 8, 1941, the day after the bombing of Pearl Harbor, met at the time that President Roosevelt was scheduled to address a joint session of Congress and ask for a declaration of war on Japan. We could hear the president's speech on the radio at Alumni Hall or at the bookstore. The professor told us that we could go and hear it if we thought we must, but that we would be counted absent from class and have the absence recorded on our records. I went, of course, and never regretted going.

For those who were alive then, Pearl Harbor—as we came to refer to the bombing—changed all our lives forever. In the fall of 1941, I still spent a good deal of time with my high school friends, and on the day of the bombing I went with some of them to a meeting of my high school fraternity. I don't know when and how I first got news of Pearl Harbor. Although a later edition told of the attack in gigantic headlines, there was nothing about it in the earlier edition of the *Tennessean,* and, until the war started, at my house we didn't usually listen to the radio in the morning. Whenever and wherever I learned of the bombing, I knew about it when I met with my friends at the Hermitage Hotel. We were a room full of boys, young men as the government judged us; we knew that each of us was going to war, and there was a sense of awe that came with knowing. Unlike later generations, we were all patriotic. It didn't occur to any of us that we shouldn't go. Even though we were ignorant of the nature of war, the agonies thereof, our love of country, our loyalty to the United States was secure. We believed, and, I suppose, all of us who remain alive still believe, that the bombing was cowardly and mean in the strongest sense of those words. But, on that Sunday afternoon, the ramifications of Pearl Harbor were more numerous and more complicated than our minds could grasp. Although we were friends of long standing, at ease in each other's company, our conversation faltered. All that we had to say could be stated in a single sentence: *We are all going to war.* Looking at each other in that room that was all but bereft of conversation, did we think of death? I believe that to the best of our abilities we did. We could look at each other and think, *Some of us will not return.* We were sincere, but on that Sunday afternoon we were incapable of confronting death for ourselves or for those closest to us. That would be realized slowly with the passing of time, when one of us died on Guadalcanal, when another's plane was shot down over the Mediterranean.

Shortly after the United States entered the war, I tried to enlist in the Army Air Corps. In an effort to strengthen my eyesight before I went for the physical examination, I took vitamins and drank carrot juice and I can't remember what other concoctions, all to no avail. After I failed the Air Corps exam, I joined the marine V-12 program, which, as it turned out, let me remain at Vanderbilt until the end of my sophomore year. Except for my English courses and, particularly, my writing courses, I didn't care much about being in school, so I did nothing to modify the poor work habits that I had developed. We were on the quarter system then, and Donald Davidson taught a course he called Advanced Composition for the first two terms of the academic year. During the second and third terms he taught Creative Writing. Knowing that I would leave Vanderbilt for the marines at the end of my sophomore year, Mr. Davidson allowed me to enroll in the second term of Creative Writing in the spring of 1943.

The first piece of writing I ever published was a story that I wrote for Mr. Davidson's Creative Writing class. Richmond Beatty, who taught American literature, compiled an anthology of the work of Vanderbilt writers that included stories by two undergraduates, one of which was

"The Lady and the Cat." Strangely, after more than sixty years, I remember writing that story, the circumstances of it, the feel of it, more vividly than I can recall writing many other things that I have written since. I wrote the story the night before it was due, not because I had been dilatory but because I couldn't find an idea that I could make work as a story. I thought of the woman and the little boy and the cat, but I had no idea what I could do with them. I took a walk, cherishing the darkness between streetlights, trying to think, but not thinking in any organized way. I wish I could say exactly how I felt that night—a mixture of confidence and uncertainty, a sense that I could write a story, but no inkling of whether it would be any good or where the plot would go. When I got home, I wrote it without interruption, and Mr. Davidson liked it. I'm certain that he, and not Dick Beatty, selected it for the anthology. I wasn't conscious of what the story was trying to get at. I still don't know, but there it is.

Eleanor Ross, a graduate student from North Carolina, was Mr. Davidson's assistant in 1943. She had been an undergraduate at what was then the Woman's College at Greensboro, North Carolina, where she had met and become friends with Allen and Caroline Tate. The Tates had moved to Monteagle. They invited Eleanor to spend the Easter weekend with them, and Eleanor invited me to come too and told me which of my manuscripts to bring for the Tates to look at. On the way up the mountain, Eleanor and I sat at the back of the bus, and she read over my stories and corrected spelling errors that she had missed when she had read them earlier. When we got to Monteagle, there was Allen Tate. Besides Mr. Davidson, Allen was the first real writer I had ever met. There he was, a dapper little man with a large head and a small mustache. Allen drove us to his house on the Monteagle Assembly grounds, and there was Caroline, small too, and not at all as dapper as Allen. Allen had wonderful taste in clothes; Caroline might have had good taste too—how was a mere male to know?—but I never thought that she had Allen's kind of vanity. She was proud of her work, and jealous of any other fiction writer whom she considered to be her competition. Like Allen, Caroline was deadly serious about literature. Both would spend their time and their energy trying to help young writers whom they considered worth helping, and they read my manuscripts and talked to me about them that weekend.

Robert Lowell, "Cal" to everybody who knew him, and his then wife, Jean Stafford, he a poet, she a novelist, were living with Allen and Caroline. Except that he was big and raw boned and looked powerful, Cal was a poet from central casting. His hair was seldom combed, his clothes didn't seem to fit, and his heavy spectacles were often not quite straight on his nose. Jean, like Caroline, was a little dowdy. She smoked too much—later she had emphysema—and seemed to have a mercurial disposition. Cal had recently become a Catholic, and, I think, he had dragged Jean with him into the church. He was an enthusiastic Christian. This was before Vatican II, when Catholics fasted all the weekdays of Lent, and Eleanor and I arrived on Good Friday. Cal and Jean had gone to church that day, and they would go again on Sunday while the rest of us recovered from our Saturday night debauchery. Later, Cal would serve a term in federal detention for claiming to be a conscientious objector and refusing to go to war. In 1943, he was free to write poetry. That night he read aloud from his work in progress. His poetry was dense. When I saw it on the page, I often could not understand it. Allen could, and I saw that night the first of hundreds of demonstrations of Allen's brilliance, his intellectual skill. Apparently, from hearing Cal read his poem, probably many times, Allen had almost memorized it, line by line. He caught every change that Cal had made, a word here, a phrase there, and told Cal whether the changes were good or bad. Cal listened intently. Later he would make a point of moving away from Allen's influence, as he should have done, but at Monteagle he was a good and grateful student.

I talked first to Caroline about my stories. She advised me to use the names of the speakers in passages of dialogue, and she accused Hemingway of corrupting my whole generation with his blunt, parsimonious style. The title of one of my stories was "Only the Brave," and Allen warned me not to choose romantic titles or titles that promised more than the story would deliver. Caroline was writing *Women on the Porch;* fearful that the house would burn in her absence, she took the manuscript with her wherever she went. Fannie Cheney, whom I knew slightly as the reference librarian at Vanderbilt, arrived on Saturday and almost immediately began to read Caroline's manuscript. I tried to read it too, but the manuscript was long and I was diverted by the other visitors—by Peter Taylor, who had come to Monteagle from Fort

Oglethorpe, where the army had sent him, and by James Waller, a political scientist who taught somewhere in the east. Peter was twenty-six and would soon launch his career with some incredibly good stories. He was very nice to me that weekend, which was a tribute to his breeding. For the rest of his life, whenever the occasion arose, he told me that he hated me when we first met because he thought I was dating Eleanor, with whom he had fallen in love at first sight. Six weeks later, Eleanor and Peter were married at St. Andrew's chapel near Monteagle with Cal as Peter's best man and with Allen giving away the bride. By the time of the wedding, to which I would not have been invited in any event, I had left for the marines. I was in Chapel Hill, North Carolina, still feeling the glow of that glorious weekend.

Chapter Six

A Different Drummer

I received orders to leave Nashville on the last day of June 1943, along with a voucher for a railroad ticket to Durham, North Carolina, and two or three vouchers to pay for meals along the way. I don't remember that I had any deep feelings about leaving—fear, regret, anticipation. I was certain that I wanted the least possible display of emotion when I got on the train, so I arranged for a friend to drive me to the old Tennessee Central railroad station. I told everybody good-bye in the living room of the East Douglas house, got to the station in good time, and waited alone while the other boys, some of whom I had known at Vanderbilt, lingered with their families until the conductor called for us to board. Strangely, I don't remember much about the trip. It was uncomfortable; we slept in our seats and looked at the things we had brought from home, toilet kits and fountain pens and clothes that we would have to send home after we were issued our uniforms. Did we go all the way into Chapel Hill by train, or did we have other transportation to take us from Durham? I remember that it was night when we checked in with the sergeant on duty, late at night when I found the room to which I had been assigned. I took the remaining upper bunk—

three other future marines had arrived before me—but I had developed a severe cold, and lying down was misery, so for a while I walked the floor.

I was housed in Smith Hall. We had breakfast the next morning in a cafeteria near the dormitory that had been set aside for our use. We drew our uniforms, registered for our classes, and got our books. It was like being in college as a civilian except that the people in charge of us were serious and firm of purpose. Fail a course, miss classes, misbehave, and you would be shipped out as an enlisted man, which all of us feared much more than we feared the war. That we would fail to be commissioned was our only apprehension; anything else the Marine Corps wanted to do with us was of little consequence. Immediately after classes began, I had cause to worry. I did not know until I was told by the authorities at Chapel Hill—Vanderbilt for some reason never informed me—that at the end of the spring term, 1943, I had been put on academic probation. Chemistry was my undoing. I had failed the third term thereof in my freshman year, taken it again the third term of my sophomore year, and made an E, which meant that I could be reexamined and would pass the course if I passed the exam. But I had not been reexamined, and the E remained a blemish on my record.

Being on probation, I dared not falter, as I think I would have done, if my fellow marines had not been so dumb. Some of them were bright, as I was bright in some subjects, but we had a large contingent of ex-football players from Alabama and Mississippi and similar places—enough of them significantly to deplete the marine contingent should they be required to pass the basic course in physics. There were navy V-12 students at Chapel Hill, more of them than there were marines, and a good number of them also could not pass physics. The university met this threat to their enrollment by offering Physics 0, with which those students who could not pass Physics 100 could satisfy the military requirement. This took care of almost all of the naval contingent, but even a simplified course left many marines, including me, behind. Still not wanting to lose students, the physics department devised Physics M, open only to marines, and we were urged not to talk about it. Like Physics 0, Physics M would carry no credit either to transfer or to use toward graduation at Chapel Hill. I believe the courses did not go on our transcripts. But Physics M got the marines through, and, to tell the truth, we had a jolly time learning the difference between a yard and a meter or watching the professor—surely a first-year graduate student, if that—balance a Ping-Pong ball on a current of air. For me everything academic was smooth sailing after that.

I took the required course in math, and, when I applied myself, I discovered that math wasn't as difficult or as boring as I had previously thought. With physics and math out of the way, I could take English and history and philosophy. It seemed that certain professors were assigned to teach V-12 students. The same man taught all the English classes I took. He meant well, and I did well under him, but he was so dull that I can no longer recall the subjects we pursued. The history professor, Fletcher Green, knew and disagreed with Frank Owsley of the Vanderbilt history department, who had contributed to *I'll Take My Stand*, but Green was a man of good nature and did not hold me responsible for what Frank had said and written. That left Helmut Kuhn, the philosophy professor, who was one of the best and most learned teachers I ever had. He had come from Germany with his wife and two or three small children, all refugees from Hitler. Several years after the end of the war, when he had returned to Germany, I read a slim, but brilliant, book he had written on existentialism in which he conceived what became for me an unforgettable image. The existentialist, he said, takes the road to Calvary, but, when he gets there, he finds only the crosses of the two thieves.

There was another philosophy teacher available to V-12 students, a man whose last name was Mack, one of whose courses I took and with whom I sometimes drank beer, but whenever I could, I stayed with Professor Kuhn. From him I took the history of philosophy, aesthetics, and a course that he called In the Wake of Hegel. It included some Hegel, of course, and *The Communist Manifesto*, Kierkegaard's *Fear and Trembling*, the Grand Inquisitor section of *The Brothers Karamazov*, Nietzsche's *The Birth of Tragedy*, and other works in which we attempted to trace Hegel's influence, and which we tried to interpret according to Hegel's dialectical view of history and of reality itself. Was it in this course that we read *Antigone*, Hegel's favorite play and the perfect example of his theory of tragedy? Probably not, but we read it somewhere. Helmut Kuhn endowed my days at Chapel Hill with learning and joy.

Initially, my roommates in our commodious corner room were Joe, a football player from Alabama; Eddie, a football player from a small college in one of the Carolinas or Virginia; and William Alexander Stuart III, called Zan, who was descended from J. E. B. Stuart. General Stuart's portrait hung in the living room of the Stuart home in Abington, Virginia. Zan was an amiable and witty chap who once described a girl as looking like the wife of Bath because of a gap between her teeth. He had been in VMI before we were called to active duty, and he was handy to have around because he knew the ropes of military life. He wittily denigrated our efforts at close-order drill, which we were required to make for an hour or so every Thursday. Joe moved out first, joining some of his Alabama friends when one of them left to play football for the Naval Academy. Eddie moved out too, miffed because Zan and I wouldn't take his major in physical education seriously: we laughed all one afternoon after he told us that the topic under discussion in one of his classes was the best posture to assume when you were having a bowel movement. Eddie swapped rooms with Emmet, who was also from Vanderbilt and who had been assigned a room with some athletes from Ole Miss. With permission, we took the two double bunks apart, set up three of the separated bunks as single beds, and took the remaining bunk to the storeroom. It was a nice arrangement.

Emmet, long dead now from a stroke, partially caused by his disposition to do and eat and drink almost anything that wasn't good for him, was not temperamentally suited for the Marine Corps. Zan called him "the sad bull," which was an apt nickname because Emmet was big and clumsy and perpetually perturbed, usually about some situation that he himself had initiated. Like his father, who owned a truckline and, although married, had tried to date my mother, Emmet believed that the way to get ahead in the world or in the Marine Corps was to cultivate friends who would do you favors. At this time when good whiskey was difficult to find, Emmet's father tried to bribe the navy captain, commandant of the whole V-12 unit at Chapel Hill, with a case of Jack Daniel's. He wanted the captain to arrange for Emmet to enroll in law school for his last term at Chapel Hill, an effort that for whatever reason was successful. Emmet's idea of how to survive was not to shine his shoes before an inspection but to make friends with the sergeant who was going to do the inspecting.

The last time I saw him as a marine was at Quantico, where we were in officer candidate school and he was failing. He had come to my building because, as always, he wanted something out of the ordinary, this time something from the armory that was in the basement of my barracks. At his request I went to the armory with him and waited while he tried, unsuccessfully I think, to get whatever it was he was after. On our way back up the steps, we met the captain of my company. We stood aside and came to attention, but Emmet really couldn't come to attention any more than he could keep his tie straight, or resist attempting to find a way that would excuse him from keeping it straight. Somehow this seemed always to be obvious, and it was obvious to Captain Linewebber that night. The captain said nothing to me, but he asked Emmet questions to which he received fumbling answers, bawled him out, and sent him on his way. The next time I heard from Emmet, we were in Nashville, and he wanted some literary quotations that would help him with a lawsuit he was trying.

Chapel Hill was where what I thought of as our honorable cheating started. We were herded through medical examinations, which were given frequently, in long lines. Each man carried his record from one doctor or corpsman to another, each of whom would mark us pass or fail in whatever part of us he was testing. Did our superiors know what we were doing? At Chapel Hill, sergeants would march us to the hospital and wait for us to go through our routine. The doctors and the corpsmen were busy with one man after another. When you had had your own record checked for color blindness, you could swap records with another marine and take his color-blindness test for him, something I did many times. If necessary, as it often was, you could urinate in another man's bottle. The authorities were more observant when we got to Quantico, or seemed to be, but I think they might have given us credit for wanting to stay in the corps and wanting to be officers. Such ruses did not always succeed, but often they did. There was the case of Pete, a Greek from Texas who was the strongest man I ever met, whose poor sight was officially noted. He went for test after test until at last he was allowed to get his commission.

In 1943, at Chapel Hill, no girls were admitted to the freshman and sophomore classes. They started somewhere else, usually at what was then the woman's college at Greensboro, where Eleanor Ross met Allen and Caroline Tate. The girls could transfer to Chapel Hill at the beginning of their junior year. This mandated a smaller number of girls than boys, which was inconvenient for the boys, but not so inconvenient as it might appear. The junior and senior girls almost never dated freshmen and sophomore boys, and although the numbers of upperclass boys and girls still didn't even out, they were closer. The administration at Chapel Hill was friendly to romance, or, some might say, licentiousness. There was the arboretum where the trees were large and the nights were dark and where no night watchman patrolled the premises. On Sunday evenings, in clement weather, there was "Music under the Stars." The gates to the football stadium were unlocked, no lights burned, and romantic music was played over the public address system. Couples brought blankets and lay down on the field, and, as in the arboretum, no one came to disturb them.

While I was at Chapel Hill, I dated a girl called Smoky whose father was a professional army officer. There was not much to do in Chapel Hill except listen to the music on Sunday night and admire the trees, which Smoky and I did when we had the opportunity. There were a few places to buy beer, a few very undistinguished eating places, a movie theater, and an occasional party sponsored by the university. Smoky and I talked about literature; we talked about philosophy; we talked about the progress of the war and how soon I might get to it. As I have said, this was a strange time. In her Civil War memoir written long after the war had ended, Sarah Rice Prior said that for those in the South who had lived through it, the war was the only reality, that all that came before and all that came after was like a dream. Almost a hundred years later few of us shared the intensity of Mrs. Prior's feelings, but even for those who were least affected by it, our war years are set apart in our memories, different from the rest of our lives.

For those who were young, at least, nothing seemed permanent. Boys knew that they were not likely to stay in any place very long. Orders would come, and they would have to leave, to go to the next post or to a boat that would take them where there was fighting. Friends had difficulty keeping up with one other. When men went home on leave their friends were no longer there. Nothing seemed to be the same as it had been when they left, so they often felt like strangers in the houses where they had grown up and among the people whom they had known all their lives, even members of their own families. And always there were the chronicles of the dead. Evidence of mortality was everywhere, in the small pictures of the deceased that appeared in newspapers and at the railroad stations where bodies in wooden boxes were stacked on carts waiting to be sent home. Not every family lost a loved one, but everyone, including those who were themselves in training to fight, lost somebody whose death somehow changed the terms of existence. This feeling affected my relations with Smoky more than it had informed my courtship with Jean in Nashville. Maybe it was just my uniform, which was a perpetual reminder of where I was and where I might be going. But for Smoky and me and for all of our Chapel Hill contemporaries, even though we were far from it, the war was real.

Emmet and I and Jim, who lived in the room next to ours in Smith Hall, rented a room on Franklin Street above a block of stores. The room was furnished with a double bunk, three small tables, and three straight chairs. Jim and I took our portable typewriters—Emmet, who couldn't type, sometimes asked me to type his papers for him—and although we stopped studying to talk from time to time, when we were working we kept our silence. Sometimes one of us would spend the night in the room. There was no bed check in the dormitories, so we wouldn't be missed as long as we were in formation early the next morning. I didn't like to spend the night in the room because our alarm clock was not wholly trustworthy. It kept time, and went off when it was set to go off, but if you weren't up when the alarm ran down, you were in trouble. We must not have paid much rent. As privates, we made fifty dollars a month. Emmet had more because in his letters and telephone calls home he always claimed he was sick and needed money to buy medicine.

A boy, a civilian, about our age rented a room across the hall from us, not for a place to study but for a place to entertain women, which, I suppose, was the reason he was not very neighborly. If we encountered him, he would speak to us grudgingly if he was alone and not at all if a girl was with him. I saw his point. The war caused public and private morals to deteriorate, but it was still daring for a girl to be alone with a boy in a bedroom. The boy in the other room had a record player of the type we had then. You stacked records on a spindle. When one finished playing, the record above it would drop and play until you got to the last record, which would play repeatedly until you cut off the machine or turned the stack of records over. One afternoon, I heard music coming from the room across the hall, which was not strange because we often heard our neighbor's records. But then I noticed that the same song, Benny Goodman's recording of "These Foolish Things," was playing over and over, and since a boy and a girl were alone in the room and neither of them was changing the records or cutting off the machine, it was hard to avoid drawing conclusions about what they were doing.

The boy often played this record. I myself had played it on jukeboxes. I had listened to it in the Sigma Nu house at Vanderbilt. I had heard it so often that I almost knew by heart what notes were going to be played. I remembered that I had heard the music live when Benny Goodman played in Nashville, and the music invoked a feeling of nostalgia for that other time, for the other life I had lived, for the other people I had known. The nostalgia was built on innocence. In spite of the strangeness I had sometimes felt on my visits home, I assumed, without considering why I should assume it, that when the war was over, I would go home again to the sort of life I had lived before I left. There would be the same things to do and the same people to do them with; the best of my memories seemed the truest, and I ignored all the past that had caused me pain. I don't think I was alone in my belief that the future would reprise the best of the past. There was no way to know how different the future would be. So I mused about the past and felt sad. Then Jim came in and slammed the door and ended my reverie. He was angry with Emmet and me about something. Jim was moody, of capricious temperament, and we soon knew why: his brother, a captain in the Marine Corps, had been killed on Tarawa.

I was still at Chapel Hill, still occupying the corner room with Zan and Emmet, on June 6, 1944. I don't know who owned the radio we listened to—it wasn't mine—or who turned it on that morning, but the invasion of France had begun, and the reporter was broadcasting from a ship in the English Channel. We could hear the heavy sound of navy guns and occasionally the sound of automatic weapons. It was impossible then to know what was happening. We knew only that the invasion was underway, and we assumed that it would succeed, but we had no facts on which to base that assumption. Our room began to fill with other marines who had come to listen. There were many other radios on our floor, and at least some of them were turned on, but for reasons that none of us tried to articulate we seemed to want to be together. We didn't talk. We waited and listened; we listened and waited. In the little military training that we had had, we had been taught to disdain whatever the army undertook, but the invasion was an army undertaking and we were mesmerized by the unimaginable scale of it. We tried to conceive of how many lives it would cost to establish such a gigantic beachhead. Although some of the battles the marines had fought and would fight—Iwo Jima, Okinawa—had been and would be bloody beyond belief, compared to the invasion of France they were like private little wars, the theaters circumscribed by the dimensions of the islands.

In our room in Smith Hall, we continued to remain quiet and to listen: to the sound of gunfire from three thousand miles away, to the voice of the reporter who, like us, was unable fully to comprehend what he was attempting to describe. I do not know what my fellow marines were thinking. In those hypnotic moments the sounds that came from the radio seemed not to break but to reinforce our silence. As the invasion continued, I tried to feel a kind of empathy for those who were dying at Normandy, but no such empathy is possible. No one knows or could know what it was like except those who were there. In our room we stayed with our radio as long as we could, but, at Chapel Hill, D-day was not a holiday. We had classes to attend, and we left to attend them, walking across the campus in small groups, carrying our books as usual, but in my case, at least, no longer feeling like ordinary college students. Our concept of what we had been doing for the last year and what we might be doing in the year to come had been altered.

In less than a month, most of us who had gathered to hear the news of the European invasion would be marching at Parris Island.

Chapter Seven

The Real Marines

At the end of June, we left by train for Parris Island. There were other marines from other colleges already aboard when we got on the train; others boarded later as we made a slow progress to South Carolina. We stopped at a railroad yard at Beaufort and saw still other marines on other trains, all of us looking out the windows, standing on the observation decks trying to assess the unknown ambience that we were entering. We were met by marine sergeants who made it clear that they considered us a sorry bunch, not good enough to warrant their attention. We left the trains and crossed the tracks conscious of how different we looked and were from the NCOs who awaited us standing straight in their tailored shirts and their wide-brimmed campaign hats that, from our point of view at least, set them apart from the rest of humanity. We wore our fore-and-aft caps that in the Marine Corps were universally called "piss cutters." We pulled ourselves into the open trucks that waited for us and were told to move back, move back, until we were pressed together as tightly as we thought we could get, and still the sergeants pushed more of us in. Finally, when the sergeants were satisfied that the truck was as full as it could get, they draped a tarpaulin over its stake sides, and we rode in the July, South Carolina, heat for what seemed an eternity.

At Parris Island, we got off, fell into an imperfect formation, and waited in the sun while a sergeant laughed at us. "Anybody here from Tennessee?" the sergeant asked.

Emmet immediately said he was, sensing that some preferment might be made of this, trying to curry favor with the sergeant.

"Don't you wish you were back there?" the sergeant said. Nobody laughed. But, perhaps with the exception of Emmet, we all got the message: don't answer anything that you were not forced to answer.

When the sergeant finished laughing at us, he marched us to a barbershop, where the experienced barbers quickly shaved our heads. We were made to shower, then we were marched—if that is the proper designation for our clumsy efforts—to the quartermaster. We already had uniforms, but only those parts of uniforms that were consonant with the relatively posh life that we had so far led. Now we drew rough leather shoes, issued a size larger than we claimed to wear. I don't know what the quartermaster called these on his inventory; to everyone else in the corps they were "boondockers." We got packs, entrenching tools, shelter halves—two used together made a pup tent for two men, and they could be used for ponchos. We got jungle hats that some of us would knock off with our rifles when we started drilling. We were ordered to remove the globe-and-anchor insignias that we had worn at college. We were not real marines and wouldn't be until we finished boot camp—if we finished it, which our sergeants doubted that any of us would do. Next we went to the armory and drew new M-1 rifles—never to be called a gun—that were still half covered with cosmoline, a heavy rust-preventing grease that we had to remove with a solvent the armorer gave us and any rag or brush that we could find. I used a toothbrush that I had a hard time replacing since we were not allowed to go the Post Exchange or anywhere else except the mess hall if we weren't marched there.

We were housed in Quonset huts constructed of galvanized metal and shaped like half a gigantic barrel turned on its side. An aisle ran down the middle; on each side there were single bunks—I don't recall how many, at least six, perhaps eight. Along the way, we had drawn footlockers that we placed at the ends of our bunks. My hut housed a jolly group, profane and vulgar, but not one of whom had been with me at Chapel Hill. We were all strangers to one another—whether by chance assignment or by design, I never knew. We soon became friends, if for no other reason than out of sheer necessity. We lived together, worked together, ate together, complained to each other; this was our only pastime except for talking about sex. We were platoon number 432. We wore dungarees, green pants and jackets with our names stenciled on them, so the sergeants and corporals could curse us individually as well as collectively. We said "sir" to all noncommissioned officers and sprang to attention when one entered our hut.

We had no hair to comb, but we were required to shave closely every day, and that was a problem. In the nautical language we were required to use, a bathroom was a "head," and ours was a wooden building without lights. I don't know whether it was not wired for electricity or whether the power had been cut off, but, although light came through small windows when the sun had risen, every morning we had to shave in the dark. We fumbled our ways to one of the sinks, trying to remember where they were from our last sight of them in the daytime. We shaved by touch, and we often cut ourselves, which was all right unless the cut marred our appearance, which would get us in trouble. We learned quickly that our inability to see in the darkness would not excuse us. Whatever went wrong in our performance was our fault, even if it wasn't. One morning at inspection, the drill instructor accused a boy of having failed to shave. The boy declared that he had shaved as best he could in the dark, and I'm sure he had. The drill instructor said, "Lad, you didn't shave this morning. If you tell me again that you did, I'll run you up," which meant putting him on report to the captain.

Parris Island is all sand except where it is paved, and our huts were built in rows with a space of sandy ground between them. Two sidewalks so narrow that two people could not pass on them ran along in front of the rows of huts. We were required to keep the sand around them raked and smooth and free of footprints, which was an impossible task and kept us constantly in trouble. Every morning we were awakened by the impatient voice of our sergeant. "Four thirty two," he would say, "get out of those God damned fart sacks!" We rose without hesitation and, like characters in the Bible, we picked up our mattresses, held them over our heads, ran to the designated space at the end of the huts, and fell in in a ragged formation. Our drill instructor checked to see that none of us had escaped during the night, swore at us for a while, then dismissed us to run back to our huts. The rule in boot camp was that we ran everywhere, which was one of the ways that we were different—meaning better—than other branches of the service. Often we saw army training films that had been selected to demonstrate the difference between us and them. When they were told to fall out, which was our signal to sprint to our huts, they made a leisurely progress to their barracks. Their obstacle courses were easier than ours; the scores they were required to make to qualify with a weapon were not as high as ours. In a short time, training films, theirs and ours, and the constant admonitions of our superiors convinced us that we individually and as a group would be superior soldiers.

At Parris Island we did calisthenics and learned how to march, both of which required us to use our rifles. The M-1 weighs slightly more than nine pounds. It could be used as a kind of weight to be raised and lowered time after time, usually after we had finished push-ups and knee bends and other exercises. Almost always, we did these in deep dry sand. After the morning formation that required mattresses, we fell out with our rifles, marched with our rifles, learned to do with our rifles whatever we were commanded to do. We learned to take our rifles apart and put them back together, and we learned the names of all the parts. We had pieces of heavy cord, a foot or so long, called "tie-ties" that we used to make loops on the sides of our bunks to hold our rifles when we weren't carrying them. We also used tie-ties as clothespins to hold our dungarees and underwear on the line after we had washed them in our standard-issue buckets. Most important of all, we kept our rifles clean. To do this in that sandy world, we needed small paintbrushes that we got from somewhere, most likely from kind parents. An even slightly dirty rifle earned you a stint on KP, during which the mess sergeants would make you scrub the floor and clean the enormous, free-standing pots and scour the still-hot metal cooktops with steel wool and scrub the garbage cans. If we were lucky we might be made to peel potatoes, but that was a chancy business that might get us into further trouble. Every mess hall had a potato-peeling machine that didn't peel but ground the peelings away with its rough interior surface. The human potato peelers had to remove the potato eyes by hand. We were tempted to leave the potatoes in the machine until the eyes were ground off, in which case the potatoes would come out of the peeler not much bigger than marbles. The mess sergeant would have his vengeance by giving us more KP that might require us to get out of bed an hour or two before reveille.

Parris Island is a few miles north of Savannah, Georgia. When the temperature reached one hundred, someone raised a flag that meant we were not to drill until the heat moderated. The raised flag only made our situation worse. We usually drilled on a large asphalt drill field. When the flag went up, our instructors took us behind our huts and drilled us in the loose sand. I'm sure that the senior officers must have known what the drill instructors were doing. The flag was a tool like the army training films: we were marines, and heat wouldn't stop us. I don't know. Possibly the senior officers believed they could protect themselves with the orders they had issued should one of us die of heatstroke. In my platoon, nobody died. We accustomed ourselves to this unaccustomed life, learned not to cut ourselves shaving in the dark, gauged how fast our hair was growing back by feeling our scalps, saw ourselves only in silhouette when the sun cast our shadows on the spotless white sand. After a few weeks, we were allowed occasionally to go to the PX, but here my memory is vague. I remember the building. I remember that we went to the PX in small groups, were given limited time to shop, and were allowed to buy ice cream if we could eat it fast enough.

Working in the PX was the kind of job a W.R., as the women marines were called, would normally have. I think I would remember if one had worked there, because I do not recall seeing a single woman for all the time I was at Parris Island, and I missed them dreadfully. Of course, we talked about them in the huts. We talked about them individually and in general. We told lies about our exploits. But that was something else. I missed the company of women, the sight of their faces, the sound of their voices, their gestures, their subtlety—all the things that made them attractive beyond mere prurient desires. Mail from girls should have helped, and in a way it did, but in another way it didn't. The letters were often fragrant, the handwriting was open and feminine; they spoke of love and the past, what we had done together and what we might do in the future. But there was little they could say about the present, because we had no common present to talk about. Like our relatives, the girls who wrote to us remained in a world that we had left, an ambience to which, at best, we would not return until the war was over. Our quotidian experiences were too different for us quite to communicate with each other; the common emotional attraction that we had once felt had somehow been damaged.

We claimed to hate our drill instructors—DI was the usual way to refer to one—and one day we were amused when our sergeant displayed a splendidly swollen and discolored eye. I think it was hurting him. He had arrived at reveille wearing sunglasses. At midmorning, he announced that he was going to remove his glasses, and he threatened us with every punishment available in the Marine Corps plus our own punch in the eye from him if any of us laughed. Under such duress, we contained our merriment, but when we were dismissed that night, even the topic of girls was neglected in our happy conversation about the sergeant's eye. Yet slowly, in spite of the agony that he put us through, we were developing—what? Not empathy and not affection, although we were gaining affection for one another. Respect, to be sure, but there was something else; whatever we felt remains for me an undefinable relationship.

We continued to drill and to do push-ups in the sand, and the time came for us to go to the rifle range. We had known from the beginning that we would go there sooner or later, and we expected, rightly, that our stint there would mitigate our boredom and be less demanding physically than drill and calisthenics. Without being conscious of doing so, we listened for the sound of small-arms fire that we heard emanating from the range every day, the noise reduced by distance to a rumble. We marched to the armory to have firing pins installed in our heretofore disabled rifles. We packed our gear, climbed aboard trucks—these more comfortable and less crowded than those we had ridden from the railroad yard—arrived on schedule, and found our assigned quarters, which were large tents, each with four or maybe six cots. That first day, we were shown where things were—the mess hall, the heads, and, most important of all, the shed where we were to clean our rifles, the rows of sinks, the vats of whale oil. Early the next morning, we went to the range, heard a lecture or two, and did a lot of dry firing.

The M-1 rifle is gas operated, as almost all small arms were then and still are, I suppose. Part of the gas created by the explosion of the cartridge is used to move the bolt back, extract the now empty casing, cock the rifle, strip another cartridge from the clip, and load it in the chamber. Dry firing, done without ammunition, was a two-man operation. One man sat in a firing position, aimed the rifle, and pulled—or more properly, squeezed—the trigger. The other man knocked the bolt back with the heel of his hand. The rifle would once more be cocked and the first man could once more aim and once more release the trigger. I did not think that this exercise was very valuable because it did not give you a proper feel of the rifle. The pushing back done by hand is similar to a recoil, but because some of the gas from the shot is dissipated in the operation of the bolt, the M-1 lifts upward without exerting much, if any, backward force. And, of course, dry firing was boring whether you were aiming the rifle or cocking it for someone else. Instructors lectured us about gun safety: at all times we were to treat every firearm as if it was loaded. We were never to point any rifle or pistol at somebody unless we intended to shoot him. We were forbidden in the strongest terms to take ammunition away from the range. If we had ammunition in our possession, we would be court-martialed.

At the range, my tent was next to that of two of the instructors, which was a mixed blessing. The sides of all our tents were rolled up against the August heat, so we could hear music from the instructors' radio, the first we had heard in more than a month. Like letters from home, but in a different way, the voice of Frank Sinatra was greatly satisfying after my long separation from any music, but it was also a reminder of a time that was no more. As I have said, most of us were innocent then— not only marines in boot camp, but soldiers and sailors and the people at home. We did not dream that the world as it existed on Pearl Harbor day was gone forever. Foolishly, we thought that the war would end, and we would take up our lives at the points where we had left them, and that our lives would continue in the same way that they had gone before. But being wrong about the future is no antidote for nostalgia or loneliness. So I listened to Frank Sinatra singing "This Love of Mine" and remembered that in the fall of 1941 this record was played in every Vanderbilt fraternity house that I visited; you could hear it in the bookstore and in your car. Between songs, I listened to the marine instructors talking. Theirs was some of the most obscene conversation I ever heard.

On the rifle range, we fired at targets from various distances: 100, 300, and 500 yards. Later, in problems we ran at Camp Lejeune, we would fire at human-shaped targets that popped up suddenly in unexpected places and crossed in front of us or at an angle. To suit our amateur skills, the targets at Parris Island were the usual shape—a bull's eye with circles around it—and they did not move. The targets were operated by marines who occupied the "butts," a trench from which they raised and lowered the targets. They marked the holes the bullets made with squares of black or white tape by which the instructors could calculate the shooter's score for that round of firing. The men in the butts waved a red flag, known as "Maggie's drawers," to indicate that a bullet had completely missed the target. We fired from various positions; standing was the most difficult because it was almost impossible to hold the rifle still when you had nothing on which to rest it. In the prone position, both elbows rested on the ground. An elbow was propped on a knee in the sitting position, and the shooter got further support from the rifle sling. There was also a kneeling position. I thought the use of the sling, although valuable for those who shot in competition, was useless for combat training. In the time that it took to kneel and adjust your sling, you could be shot and found dead and be on your way home to whoever wanted you.

At the end of our training, there was a final examination held at the range in which we fired from various positions and from different distances. Your level of skill was judged according to the score you made on the final day. Everyone was expected to "qualify" with the M-1, and there were three levels of competence for which different badges were issued. Marksman was the lowest level; it was simply to qualify. The middle level was sharpshooter. The highest was expert. In all our preliminary trials, I shot expert. The day before our last day at the range, an NCO whom I didn't recall ever having seen before came among us at our tents and asked us what we had shot on the final round of practice. Then he predicted the levels at which we would qualify: except for those who had almost perfect scores and would become experts, he forecast that those who had shot ordinary expert scores would be sharpshooters, while those who had practiced as sharpshooters would simply qualify. Only the finest marksmen would be experts. To the chagrin of most of us, he was right. My own case was most embarrassing. All through our training, we had been warned against "buck fever," a term the military borrowed from hunters or hunters appropriated from the military that meant the shooter jerked his shoulder against the butt of the rifle at the moment of firing. I did this, I suppose out of nervousness, for the first and only time on the last day. The movement was involuntary, but I knew the moment I did it that I had ruined my score. I had also demonstrated that the confidence my instructor had in me was misplaced. When the patches on the target were one short of the number of rounds I had fired, he demanded a recount. Then I got my first and final Maggie's drawers. So, to my eternal chagrin, I finished as a sharpshooter, as the sergeant had foreseen.

Back at the main base, our days became more interesting, if not easier. We had learned close-order drill well, and we took pride in our competence. Our lines were straight; our responses were crisp; we moved our rifles from position to position while marching in almost perfect unison. We did fancy formations, spreading out the squads and marching them back together. It was now, I think, that we began to discover the purpose of all the misery our instructors had made us endure. We could do things that we could not do when we arrived at boot camp. We could shoot. We could march. In our last two or three exercises in the boondocks, inexperienced as we were, we were still vastly better soldiers than we had been at the beginning of our training. We would get even better. Later at Lejeune and then at Quantico, we would learn things that we hadn't thought about at Parris Island. At Lejeune, we were warned not to detail strip our rifles, because in removing the ejector spring we were likely to lose it. It would come out of the bolt—I would say like a bullet, but that would be an egregious image—and it would have to be put back where it belonged with a lot of force, but that was a part of the joy of it. I always caught mine with my pillow. We learned to fire a light machine gun at what was called "the thousand-inch range." I assume this was an accurate measurement of the distance between shooter and target, and I guess "thousand-inch range" is better than "eighty-three-and-a-third-foot range," or "twenty-seven-and-seven-tenths-yard range," but why did we work so close to the targets with machine guns and so far away from them with rifles?

We finished Parris Island with pride. We had a final review in which we displayed our marching skills. Our globe-and-anchor insignias were returned to us, which indicated that we were now true marines. In contrast to our ride from the railroad yard eight weeks earlier, steps were provided to ease our climb into the trucks that would return us to the mainland. On our final day at Parris Island, someone took up a collection, a present for our drill instructors, and I gladly contributed. This was a tradition about which we had heard, and in the hard first weeks of our training almost everyone had sworn not to give a nickel to our torturers. I suppose that in some platoons men honored that vow. In his memoir, my friend Chuck, who was in a different platoon from mine, says that his outfit collected so little money for their instructors that the instructors refused to accept it. Although to my knowledge nobody ever said so, I think that most of us understood that the misery we had endured had a purpose, and to a certain extent, at least, the purpose had been achieved.

When we boarded our trains to go to Camp Lejeune, most of us were proud of ourselves and almost as disdainful of what we had been eight weeks ago as our sergeants were when we first arrived on the island.

Chapter Eight

The Real Marines—Part II

At Lejeune, we lived in two-story brick barracks, our quarters in long wings at each end of the building. The large rooms at the ends were connected by corridors with offices on the first floor, heads and a few private rooms for the NCOs on the second. We slept in double-decker bunks, one row on each side, hung our good uniforms on coatracks that ran between the rows of bunks, and kept everything else we owned in our footlockers. The mess hall was a short way from the barracks. We ate off metal trays, as we had at Parris Island, but there were bowls of food on the tables for seconds and aluminum pitchers of coffee, which in the Marine Corps was called Joe. We scrubbed and polished our barracks and our equipment every Friday night, preparing for Saturday inspection; if all went well, we were allowed to have liberty on the weekends. During the week, we attended classes, where we stripped and reassembled weapons and heard lectures about squad and platoon and company tactics and ran problems in the field. The marines had built bleachers on hilltops and in clearings near where we ran our exercises, where we could sit and be told all the things we had done wrong and the few things that we had done correctly. Once, when the weather was still warm, we were caught in a rainstorm. When we sat on the bleachers to listen to the sergeant, the sun came out brightly and our steaming dungarees created our own private cloud. Usually, we did not spend the night in the field.

The commander of our platoon was a second lieutenant named Jones, and I cannot say now why every man in the platoon hated him. When we ran our problems he was seldom present. He was not around when we fell out in the darkness of early morning. On Saturdays, he inspected our barracks, and sometimes when we were in formation he walked down our lines and looked at our rifles, but by now we had learned how to keep our rifles clean, and we gave him very little for which to reprimand us. Once a friend and I had engaged in a mock bayonet fight that left my bayonet nicked, which Lieutenant Jones called to my attention. He cautioned me not to allow my "initiative," a quality prized, or at least praised, in the Marine Corps, to get out of hand. This was probably the mildest rebuke I received in all my military service, so why should I remember it so vividly and hold it against Lieutenant Jones after sixty years? Maybe it was his mild demeanor that made us all mistrust him. He seemed too eager not to do something wrong.

We soldiered on. We returned from compass problems run at night with faces and hands scratched from crashing through the undergrowth. We learned to read maps and, except in my case, to interpret aerial photographs. Left in the woods with a map and a compass, I could find my way home, but, with only an aerial photograph from which to work, I would be lost perhaps forever. Nobody asked me why I could interpret lines drawn on paper and not renditions of reality. I suppose that my map-reading skills were judged to be sufficient for me to be an officer, but I faced serious trouble two weeks before we were scheduled to leave for Quantico. During a stint as platoon commander—we rotated roles as officers and NCOs—I reported all to be present or accounted for when we formed after dark to march to a classroom. The three squad leaders had reported the same to me, but from one squad a man was missing. This would perhaps not have been discovered had the missing man stayed in the barracks or even run and caught up with the formation. But he did neither. In his panic, he ran to the classroom and got there before the rest of us arrived.

I had no excuse for my false report. The squad leader who had reported falsely was in trouble too, but his failure did not excuse mine. This, as I knew already, but not from bitter experience, was how the military worked. I know now that the careers of many officers have been thwarted and sometimes ruined by inefficiency or betrayal by their inferiors. In my case, it was my platoon, and I was supposed to know whether or not all my men were present. I hadn't known. I had made a false report. For punishment I would likely be shipped out and be denied the chance of earning a commission. I would have to leave my friends, most of whom I trusted and many of whom I loved. My friends and I, my comrades, often said that we would forgo officer candidate school and go immediately into combat if we could go together. Now it appeared that I would be going alone to find new friends and never to be an officer. I think I was saved because Lieutenant Jones was the officer on duty. He threatened to have me dismissed from his outfit. I believed him. I assumed that he did not like me any better than I liked him, and I very well may have been right about that, but apparently he did not report me. My prejudiced judgment of him says that he was keeping his own coattails clean. He was, after all, in command of me and therefore shared in my failure. Maybe not. Maybe he was being kind. Maybe what I had done was not enough to deny me my chance at a commission. For whatever reason, I survived.

There were girls in Wilmington, where we went on weekend liberty, but we never devised a way to meet them. We would stay in the Cape Fear Hotel, rooms engaged in advance, but once we checked in, there was nothing to do but use the civilized bathrooms and stretch out on beds larger than our bunks. So we drank. Sometimes we would start at lunch and then stay in the restaurant when we had finished eating in order to continue drinking. In the mellowness of midafternoon, the sun lower in the sky, the day passing faster than we thought was right, I would feel like a character out of a Scott Fitzgerald novel. I was content, happy. All discontents were ameliorated when I had drunk the right amount, although the right amount varied from weekend to weekend, and none of us ever had sense enough or control enough to stop drinking long enough fully to enjoy our moments of contentment. We kept going until we were giddy and foolish, and we staggered out of the restaurant to be surprised by what was to us a sudden twilight.

The marines at the base, and I suppose everywhere else in the Marine Corps, consisted of innocents such as my comrades and I and of those who had been in the Pacific and had been sent back to the States because of sickness or wounds. The two groups usually came together only in the "slop chutes," the enlisted mens' clubs that served beer. Even there, the different groups sat apart, the veterans at their own tables at which the rest of us would not have presumed to try to sit. There was no way for us to imagine what they had experienced, but now and then we would see one of them moving slowly down a company sidewalk, supporting himself with a cane. Once, when we were riding the bus back from Wilmington, a marine had an attack of malaria that sent him into paroxysms of shivering more violent than any I had ever seen. He was brutally sick, tormented by his chills. He leaned forward, supporting his head in his hands, and, when his chills had passed, he seemed to be made equally miserable by fever. He never uttered a sound—not a groan, not a complaint, not a prayer. He endured his hell alone and with what I thought was dignity.

For me, fighting forest fires was one of the most unpleasant tasks we had at Lejeune. Except for once when we had watched a demonstration of close air support, and the fire had been set by the fifty-caliber bursts from the airplanes, we started the fires ourselves with tracer bullets from our own machine guns. Because we couldn't begin to fight a fire until we had finished our problem, the fire would get a good start and be augmented by further rounds of tracers. We had no water except for that in our canteens. We fought the fire with picks and shovels and brooms and axes. We sweated and breathed smoke. We cursed and chopped and dug. We threw dirt on the flames remembering the rifles and machine guns and BARs that we would have to clean before we got supper.

Some aspects of our training were left to our imagination. We got a little experience shooting bazooka rockets with dummy warheads at a tank that went back and forth in front of us. The tank moved slowly, but hitting it still required some practice. These early rockets left the tube so slowly that you had to brace yourself so the weight of them wouldn't spoil your aim by pulling the front of the bazooka down. Although I kept in mind that my rockets were duds, I was still mildly disappointed that when I was able to hit the side of the tank there was only the clunk of metal hitting metal: no explosion, no hole in the tank, nothing sufficiently impressive to warrant self-congratulation. On some problems, there weren't even real tanks, or weren't supposed to be. One afternoon, I was assigned to take a position over a hill from the rest of our platoon and, on a signal from our sergeant, run back and announce that I had sighted enemy armor. The tank was to be imaginary, and I would be signaled when to give word of it. I took my position, and immediately a decrepit old tank came rumbling over the next hill down the road I was watching. Concluding that the actual tank should take precedence over the imaginary tank, I ran to warn of its coming.

The sergeant was livid. He had given no signal for me to spread the alarm, and he was still cursing me for a damned fool who was too dumb to follow orders when the tank came over the hill and rendered him speechless. This was a delicate moment. Somebody was bound to laugh. When the first person laughed the rest of us would laugh, which would most likely further infuriate the sergeant. Our immediate futures hung in the balance. Would the sergeant cancel our liberty? Would he give us extra duties? Would we have to spend the weekend scrubbing pots and cutting the eyes out of potatoes? No. His sense of humor triumphed over his feeling of personal outrage. To save face, he turned his wrath on the tank and its occupants, cursing both the machine and the men, but the tank was indifferent, and the men, surrounded by the noise that the tank made, couldn't hear him. We started over again. I returned to my advanced post to await orders to signal that tanks were coming. The other men took up their positions. We ran our problem, but without much panache. Our amusement had dissipated our fighting spirit.

Although we ran problems with blank ammunition, most of us had trouble staying alive. We were opposed by veterans who knew about actual fighting, and because they ran the same problem against succeeding classes, they knew their tactics and the terrain well. Once I was on point, out ahead of the rest of the platoon, when a machine gun, unseen by me or by any of my comrades, began to fire; if we had been fighting and not playing a game, I would have been a cadaver. It seemed to me then and still does that I was getting killed on a regular schedule. Whatever lesson I learned from one death usually was not adequate to protect me from the next. Once, when we were attacking up a hill, a man stepped out from behind a tree and shot me. This taught me to be wary of what might lurk behind trees, but the next time there was nobody behind the tree. I was killed by a sniper in the treetop. We joked about being ghosts, all of us dead many times, but returned to life to be killed again. We did not speak of ourselves as resurrected.

Who were these fellow marines of whom I was so fond? It seemed to me that the corps consisted largely of Catholics from the North and good ol' boys from the South. That was true at least of our company. All of us had been in the V-12 program; we had come from different universities, the institutions chosen I know not how. We came from Vanderbilt and Chapel Hill and Duke, from VMI and Maryland and Yale. I've wondered from time to time how close we would have been, how fond of each other, had we met in civilian life as workers at the same company or as members of the same club. We were drawn together by our common experience, our common expectations, the difficulties of our shared situation. The differences between us were those of competence and of bravery or of foolhardiness. Athletes were better than the rest of us at running obstacle courses or crawling under wire or bouncing into foxholes. Some, often the unlikely, were good at weapons. Others were born with the dignity, the command presence, that the best officers have. Others, luckily a small group, were entranced by explosives. The happiest moments of their lives seemed to be when they were blowing things up, cutting down trees and posts with nitro-cord, blowing railroad tracks with nitro-starch, making enormous craters in the ground with TNT. Most of them seemed mesmerized, determined to be as close to the charge as possible when the explosion came, but they were good people to have around because, loving it as they did, they knew their business.

To work with explosives, we were given nonferrous tools that would not accidentally strike a spark and several firm and often repeated admonitions. I convinced myself that as long as I didn't deviate from my training, there was nothing to fear from rigging fuses and connecting charges, but like most others, I stayed wary of what improperly handled explosives could do. When the time came for us to blow a crater, we were taken to a large field and given half a dozen or more crates of TNT. The sergeant told a boy to open the crates, and, in a fit of idiocy, the boy picked up an ordinary shovel and started to hack at the first crate. Quicker to respond than even the sergeant, the men who were born to work with demolitions stopped the boy and took the shovel, but in the second or two that he had used the shovel we had all turned pale. After we had set the charge, we went to what the Marine Corps reckoned was a safe distance away from the explosion, and we were told to LOOK UP! LOOK UP! LOOK UP! when the big bang came. This was hard to do. The loud explosion and the shaking earth seemed to demand attention. I had to make myself look at the sky, which was filled with a detritus of earth and stones, much of it coming down on us. The next week, in the class following ours, a man who failed to keep his eyes raised was hit by a falling rock and killed.

In some of our classes, we had heard much of an MLR—the main line of resistance set up as a defensive position. I think this was a tactic developed in World War I, and I considered it more useful to soldiers in 1917 than to those fighting on atolls and islands. I was wrong. I came to discover that MLRs were commonly established in the Pacific. An MLR was devised with the intention of creating such interlocking fire that the defensive position would be impregnable. Machine guns were aimed so there would be no gaps between lines of fire. There were two or more aprons of wire, and mortars were zeroed in on the spaces between them. Watching the tracers from the machine guns, the dirty orange explosions of the mortar shells, I thought that surely no attackers could breach this line. But there were no attackers, no artillery to try to take out the machine guns, no soldiers creeping under the machines guns' trajectories with pipe bombs to blow gaps in the wire. Without the experience of combat, I had been killed enough times in our maneuvers to know that almost nothing ever went as it was planned.

Late one hot afternoon, after a day of running and crawling and jumping into foxholes, our company began our march back to our barracks. We were in a rough formation, but not in step, moving down what seemed to be an endless road, bored, too weary even to think of anything besides marching. I was behind Emmet, and I was tired of looking at the sweating back of his neck and his dungaree jacket that seemed ill fitted even among marines and at his poorly put together pack with the handle of his entrenching tool swinging as he walked. I thought we would get a small respite if I gave Emmet grief, so I jerked the handle of his entrenching tool. I jerked harder than I intended or Emmet was more tired than I knew. I pulled him down, and for an instant he sat on the ground with the men dividing around him, moving on.

Emmet was furious. He came after me with the entrenching tool, and I ran. I ran from our place in the middle of the formation up one side of the walking company, around the front between the troops and the officers and NCOs leading us, Emmet behind me, trying to keep his rifle sling from slipping off his shoulder, threatening with his tool, but losing ground. Were there going to be consequences for this chase, I wondered? Perhaps because Emmet was Emmet and more comical than usual in his rage, everybody was laughing. I was far enough ahead to go down the other side of the formation and slip into the line of marchers before Emmet came in sight.

Would my comrades give me away? Of course they would. They were having fun and wanted it to continue. "Here he is!" the marines where I was trying to hide shouted. But, before Emmet could find me, others took up the cry. "Here he is!" they yelled, at the front, at the back, in the middle. With his entrenching tool still at the ready, Emmet sought me up and down the line. Then he saw that he was the butt of the joke. He fell in where we had been marching, but he kept his entrenching tool ready in his hand all the way back to the barracks.

In the fall, we left for Quantico. Had we paused to think of it, as most of us didn't, we would have realized that we had learned a lot. We hadn't spent all our time in the field. There were houses for us to attack, from top to bottom if we could, streets for us to fight our way down. We had fieldstripped fifty-caliber machine guns, although I don't think we ever fired them. We had more confidence in ourselves than we had had when we arrived at Lejeune, and our sense of connection with each other had deepened. As usual, we traveled by train. We slept in our seats, ate cold food, played poker and talked and pretended that we felt no apprehension. The metal floor of our train car had no carpet, and late at night somebody told us to feel the floor. We had come from the moderate autumn of North Carolina to the cold of northern Virginia. The half of us who had been asleep felt obligated to discuss this new development, and before we slept again, we exhausted the subject. When we got to Quantico, we were not surprised by the chill in the air.

Chapter Nine

Gentlemen at Last

As always happened when we changed posts, our group that had been together at Lejeune was dispersed among other troops who had come from other places. Some were enlisted men, veterans of the Pacific, whose commanders had sent them to officer candidate school. Others, with whom we never worked, who rode in the cabs of the trucks and watched as we went through our exercises, were already officers, commissioned in the field, who had come back to receive a Quantico imprimatur. Our barracks were larger and older and I thought better built than those we had occupied at Lejeune. The rooms where we slept were big enough to accommodate several rows of bunks. The heads were bigger with more showers and lavatories and commodes, and there were rooms where the lights were allowed to stay on as long as anybody was foolish enough to stay up reading or writing letters or cleaning and polishing to be ready for the next inspection. Our training proceeded in a different mode. We ran more complicated problems. We learned more about weapons, particularly machine guns and mortars. We drilled as we had everywhere, but the emphasis was less on the platoon and more on the person who was in charge of the drilling. I was good at this. For me conducting a drill was like a performance. I had a good voice and liked to use it. I didn't mind scolding my colleagues if the drill was ragged. They didn't mind either. In the best of humor they would say, "Sully, you son of a bitch. You act like you're already an officer." Then we'd go off and drink together, usually bad beer at the slop chute.

Being good at drilling others didn't keep me out of trouble. Early on, at a regimental inspection and for reasons I don't know to this day, I presented my rifle badly, and the colonel reprimanded me and reprimanded my lieutenant, who, unlike Jones, was a capable and fair officer on whom my sloppiness reflected badly. That was the last bad thing I did, but, as the weeks passed and I wasn't given a command assignment, I began to get nervous. Every problem we ran appeared to be more complex than those that had gone before, which meant that whoever was commanding a platoon—or, as time passed, more likely a company—had more opportunities to fail. I still had not functioned at any higher rank than squad leader when we went for our stint in the field. It was bitterly cold. We had tents in which to sleep, each furnished with a wood stove, and there was wood available. Early in the night, the wood would be consumed; nobody would get up to fetch more, and the tent would become frigid. We had long wool underwear that made me itch so badly I swore I'd never wear it, but after one night in the tent sleeping in my skivvies, I pulled it on with hands that shook with cold.

In addition to our underwear, we had fleece-lined coats, heavy shirts, and gloves. Nothing we wore was equal to the weather; but, as time passed and our weariness grew, we learned to sleep under almost any circumstance. If we were marching, we would take ten-minute breaks every hour to drink water if our canteens weren't frozen, or to smoke if we could make our Zippo lighters work without taking off our gloves, or to lie on our backs with our collars pulled up around our heads and sleep with our helmets for pillows. When we made our pup tents and slept on the ground, we missed our big tents with their wood stoves. We shivered in our sleep, woke up stiff and aching, and longed for the sun to rise to loosen our joints and relieve our trembling.

Cold or not, I performed satisfactorily in the field. I did what I was commanded to do, got into foxholes the proper way, hugged the ground and kept my head down, shot at what I was supposed to shoot at. I took off my coat and gloves to fire a machine gun problem, and paid for it with hands that stayed swollen long after we had returned to our heated barracks. I shot the problem well, explaining in detail to my lieutenant where I was firing, although he could see for himself by watching the tracers, and why I was firing there. He appeared to be satisfied, but still I was given no command responsibilities.

One night I was awakened by the sobs of one of my tent mates. Actually, it was morning, not long before reveille, but I had been sleeping soundly and the darkness was profound, with no hint of daylight at the edges of the tent, no spark from the dead stove, not even a glow from the dial of my watch, which was supposed to be luminous. For a moment, I didn't know what I was hearing. I was afraid, in the way you are afraid at the moment of awaking from a nightmare when the fearful aspects of the dream are as real as the darkness. Then I was more fully awake, and I knew what the sound was and who was making it, but I was mystified and still a little afraid, as if this cry of desolation, these sobs not quite like any I had ever heard before, somehow included me. My other tent mates were awake. I could hear movement on their bunks, but for a while the weeping continued to be the only human sound in the tent. Finally, one of the men in the tent said he would go get the lieutenant. He fumbled for his clothes, taking more time than I thought he ought to take, and I began to feel that the weeping had to stop, that somebody had to do something before all of us were involved in this desperate sadness. I was relieved to hear reveille, happy, perhaps for the only time in my Marine Corps career, to have to get out of bed, to dress, to hasten to formation to begin another day of work and discomfort. We left our comrade alone in the tent, and when we returned from breakfast his bed was stripped, and he and all his belongings were gone. We were never told where he went or what happened to him, but after the war I heard from one of my friends that he had been in St. Elizabeths Hospital in Washington—the facility for the mentally and emotionally distressed where Ezra Pound was kept after his arrest for treason.

The night before we were to return to the main base, the officers gave a beer party for us in the mess hall. We could drink as much as we wanted, and we drank more than we should have and made jokes, some at the expense of the officers, but even in our cups we knew that the jokes had to be mild and only mildly disrespectful. A contingent who had been music majors at Oberlin, who often sang in the barracks after lights-out, their harmonies near perfect, the lyrics obscene, entertained us with parodies they had written of off-color songs we had heard in Washington bistros, the words changed to fit our situation. Warm and inebriated, we could laugh about our recent hardships, the cold weather, the long hours, the days without bathing or even brushing our teeth. Early the next morning, we boarded our trucks and returned to our barracks. I still had not been given a responsible command.

After another two weeks, perilously close to the end of our officer training, I got my test. I was to be captain of our company during an amphibious operation, the first that we had run. When I read the schedule, I was glad to discover that my lieutenants and most of the men who would be senior NCOs for the operation were fairly dependable. Our instructors had lectured us on landings. We had seen training films. Trying to remember everything I had heard or seen, I gathered my officers and sergeants and repeated what they probably knew as well as I knew it, but I had been given specifics, the goal of our operation and how we would attain it, which I tried to explain as clearly as possible to my officers. Our first test would be getting from the deck of the ship to our landing boats

The initial preparation for a landing is planning how to load the ship and distribute the troops in order that what will be needed first will be first to land. My job would have been harder if our company had conformed to the table of organization with mortar and machine gun sections and perhaps navy medical corpsmen and even a chaplain, but the company was reduced to three rifle platoons. I was required to see that my men took their places in the landing craft according to the weapons they were carrying and according to what they were supposed to do when we got to shore. The radio man and the runners, who would carry messages between me and my platoon commanders, would stay with me. Officers rode in the bows of the boats to lead their men. Sergeants remained in the sterns of the boats to be sure that all the troops disembarked. The first task I had was to rehearse my men at towers with cargo nets—similar to those we would use to get from our ship to our landing craft—strung down the sides. At our first run-through on the net, we were slightly out of order. I told my troops how to correct our errors, and, when I had finished, the captain who was instructing us said, "That's exactly right. You told them what I was going to say." But none of my company officers was present. I didn't know whether my good work would be reported to those who would decide whether I passed or failed.

That afternoon we boarded our ship and sailed out into the Potomac estuary, where, packed in the dank hold, we spent the night. There was water on the deck and more than water, I think, because our bunks were pushed close together and the heads were hard to reach and some men didn't try. Nobody got much sleep. The gamblers played poker and shot craps. You could read, but not for long because the light was poor, and although our Potomac sea was calm, and our vessel stationary, a few men, who had been apprehensive from the beginning, got sick. I lay in my bunk and worried about what I was going to do in the morning. Would everybody get over the side? Would some fool drop his weapon on the way down, maybe a BAR that would then be lost forever? Would my platoon commanders fail me? I had briefed them thoroughly, but one of the aphorisms by which the Marine Corps operates is that "there is always some son of a bitch who doesn't get the word."

The next morning, after a bad breakfast eaten in darkness, I formed my men on deck and watched them go down the cargo nets and into the landing craft. One or two of them forgot their instructions and held on to the horizontal instead of the vertical ropes, getting their hands stepped on. There was enough wind to stir the surface of the water; the boats bobbed and drifted slightly, but they were held close to the ship by the navy enlisted men who would take us to our landing area. Two of my men lost their grips, maybe those whose hands had been stepped on. They fell into the boats with a clatter of gear and weapons, but nothing was lost and they were not injured. The sun rose as we moved toward shore; the beach and the tree line behind it slowly emerged out of the darkness. Except for the sound of the boat engines, all was quiet. The men were still half asleep, and there was no firing of blanks or sound of bullets over our heads, no artillery shells falling on the beach in front of us. How our landing might be opposed was left to our imaginations. As they always did, according to Marine Corps lore, the sailors stopped short of the landing area and lowered the ramps in waist-deep water, and I was too inexperienced to demand that they move the boats closer.

As planned, I sent runners to my platoon commanders and to the battalion commander, who in this case was a real officer. Then I sent a second set of runners to the same places in case any of the first group got lost or, as was quite possible, decided to take a rest in the woods until the exercise ended. We made radio contact with platoons and battalion, but the radio, which may have gotten wet in the landing, functioned poorly. My runners did not betray me. They took my orders to the platoon commanders and kept me informed of where they were and what difficulties they had encountered. Shortly after our landing we were told to put on our gas masks, a ludicrous order, since no gas had been used by either side during the war. We did what we were told and struggled deeper into the woods, unable properly to see where we were going through the small eyeholes in the masks. After the all-clear came and we had moved a little way off the beach, we received word to halt our advance. I conveyed this order and asked my platoon commanders to come in for briefing. The captain, the real captain of our company, came with them.

My platoon leaders, one of whom was still wearing his gas mask, squatted around me in a small clearing. "Walker," I said to the man with the mask, "get that damned thing off. We've had the all-clear and you can't see what you're doing."

When he didn't respond immediately, I lifted the mask off his head and handed it to him. I think this impressed the captain. He listened without speaking while I briefed my officers and told them what we were to do next. After the lieutenants started back to their platoons, the captain asked me questions. Where were we? What had we done so far? What was left to do to achieve our objective? He seemed to be satisfied with my answers. Soon the exercise ended. I was wet and cold. I had not had time even to pour the water out of my shoes, but, as I boarded the truck that was to take us back to the base, my lieutenant gave me a thumbs-up, and I knew at that moment that I was going to be an officer in the Marine Corps. I was euphoric, more so than I was a few weeks later when I got my bars.

I had been right to worry about not getting a command. After our landing exercise, we ran night problems that frustrated the competent and caused ordinary soldiers to fail. Men who had not done well in their assignments heretofore were now given command of impossible operations. I must admit that our instructors were fair. They described the enemy installations and showed us on maps where they would be. The battle plan was discussed in more detail than mine had been when

I commanded during the landing. But in the darkness only the very best marines could find their way. We started out together. We knew where we were going. But some of us had to pass through thick woods; others stumbled over trip wires about which we had been warned, igniting flares that represented deadly booby traps. Units lost all semblance of organization. Individual men were scattered and out of touch with each other. Long before any of us got to our objective, and few did, we had ceased to exist as a fighting force.

On the trip back, I rode next to one of the men who had been in command of our confused maneuvering. He was a boy from Vanderbilt whom I had known slightly in that now far-off civilian world. From the beginning, he had not been very good at what was asked of him. There were probably many like him in every command, men who fell out of step, who misheard orders, who had to be reminded where not to point their rifles when they were on the firing line. He had failed long before he was given his night command, and he must have known this, or subconsciously have known it. But such knowledge did nothing to assuage his sense of loss. Like the rest of us, he had joined the marines because he wanted to be an officer in the Marine Corps. Now he rode with his body bent forward, his face in his hands. I was deeply sorry for him. I remembered the fears that had haunted me, the urgent desire that I had to be an officer, and I believed that I came as close as another person could come to knowing the extent of the pain he endured. I would have comforted him if I had known how—or maybe I wouldn't. Maybe my desire to retain my identity as one of the successful would have overcome my impulse toward sympathy. Whatever the case, I rode in silence beside him as he grieved.

Two weeks later, we picked up our new uniforms, for which we had been measured earlier. Dressed nattily in comparison to what we had worn before, we marched as enlisted men for the last time to a post theater where we received our commissions and watched as sweethearts and mothers and fathers pinned bars on the shoulders of some of our comrades. A friend and I did the honors for each other. Knowing, I suppose, how happy I was to receive my commission, my mother often said that she regretted not having been present. She thought it a shame that I had only another marine to pin on my bars. But neither then nor later did I feel deprived.

Chapter Ten

Deliverance

One afternoon, on a bus at Lejeune, I overheard one grizzled warrant officer ask another, "Where did all these second lieutenants come from?" A good question. There were too many of us to fit into the tables of organization. We filled the seats on the buses; we took up space at the bar of the officers' club; only a few—I was one—ever got a private room in the Bachelor Officers' Quarters, known as the BOQ. The answer to the warrant officer's question was to be found in the past and in the future. Past experience in island warfare proved that the casualty rate among junior officers was astronomical. E. B. Sledge wrote in his memoir of service with the Fifth Marines: "They were wounded or killed with such regularity that we rarely knew anything about them other than a code name and saw them on their feet only once or twice. . . . [O]ur officers got hit so soon and so often that it seemed to me the position of second lieutenant in a rifle company had been made obsolete by modern warfare." Our future was the invasion of Japan, where the fanatical Japanese would fight even more furiously than they had fought on the Pacific Islands. Second lieutenants were numerous because we would be needed in the battle for Japan.

At Lejeune, we lived in barracks as we had as enlisted men, but without inspections or housekeeping duties: others swept the floors and cleaned the heads. We attended classes, on military matters, of course, but also on the qualities of leadership and how to develop them in ourselves, on history, and on the nature of our enemies. As I think of it now, planning classes on the Japanese must have been difficult for our superiors. We needed to know that the Japanese were good soldiers, but it would not do to represent them as bigger than life, as giants who would have to be slain by our extraordinary efforts. Whatever our instructors could tell us, we knew already and knew it in better detail than we could learn in the classroom. Old soldiers talk, and every veteran of the real war, everyone who had charged up a beach, became old in experience. The rest of us had listened, not to generalities, or efforts to define national character, but to anecdotes about individual marines and their enemies. We had seen the scars that bullets and shell fragments made. We had heard men cry out in their sleep. We had known a few marines who had seen too much to be persuaded to tell their stories.

In one segment of our classes, we gave lectures, which I could do well, although a classmate from Philadelphia never stopped deploring my accent. One day, half in jest, but not fully, I talked about the history and tradition of the Marine Corps. This had strange consequences. We wrote short evaluations of the speeches of our colleagues. I expected to get a jeering response, and I was half right. Some of my friends who had heard me join in the numerous complaints about life in the corps wrote that I had given a sleazy performance intended to impress our instructors and that I ought to be ashamed of myself. These were quite good natured. As long as you didn't shirk your duty or cause trouble for anybody else, your comrades were willing for you to do anything you could get away with. So I caught hell in a friendly way and knew I would be teased later. The other half of the evaluations gave the speech high praise, but, even more, they showed that the writers of them had been moved by what I said. They were proud to be marines; they were proud of the tradition; I had reminded them of what they were and what was expected of them. What about me? After all my complaining, did I believe what I had said? Yes, I did, but, as some of us had learned from Hemingway, it was bad form to say so.

Our classroom training ended, and we got individual orders and were dispersed. I went to a casual company, a place for transients and those who were disabled and waiting for discharge—in short, the place for people who didn't belong anywhere else. I got a room in the BOQ and could use the company Jeep. Sometimes I drove it aimlessly around the base to alleviate my boredom. Every three or four days, I "had the duty," as we put it: I was officer of the day and had to spend the night in a room in the casual company barracks. In the diaspora of my Quantico classmates after our classroom work at Lejeune ended, one of my colleagues had become a mess officer, and he called to me one afternoon when I walked past his mess hall. "Hey, Sully," he said, "come here. I want to show you something." I went to the loading dock where he was sitting, and he held out a newspaper with bold headlines that told of Hiroshima and the atom bomb. At that moment, both he and I knew that the war would soon end and that there would be no invasion of Japan. "We're going to live, Sully," he said. "We're not going to die after all." Through no effort of our own, we had been lifted out of the valley of the shadow of death.

On VJ day, the day that Japan surrendered, I was once more officer of the day. As I recall, the news came to Lejeune in the afternoon, and immediately there was a sense of change on the post, ineffable, but real and profound. You could see it in the faces of some of the marines, a set of the mouth that was not quite a smirk, and in a bold and steady look in some of their eyes that you could feel following you as you walked past; you could see it in a sloppiness in some of their salutes, and in a few marines who had stopped saluting at all. As darkness fell, the sense of disorder on the base intensified. The crowded slop chutes that the shore patrol watched even in quiet times were not a problem. But pints and quarts of contraband whiskey appeared in every barracks. Drunk marines broke a few windows, by inebriated accident mostly, but probably some were broken by design. Some of the marines shouted aimlessly, hurling happy curses into the night. A few walked up and down the streets, simply making noise. Compared to the civilian riots that were to come later, the marines created a decorous disturbance, but that night it did not seem so to me.

I thought that, as the officer of the day, I had to do something to quiet my own people, but I was not sure what. Some of our classes had dealt with discipline, and, a few times, I had calmed one or two unruly marines and got their buddies who were a little less drunk than they to take care of them; but nobody had told us how to handle a company that got out of hand. Most of all that night I needed a sergeant to advise me, but the sergeants had better sense than I, and none was to be found. Finally, I decided to go among the troops, to walk up and down the barracks and make my presence known, but when I reached the passageway at the foot of the stairs and walked among the shouting marines, I knew that I had made a mistake. Most of these men had been in combat. While I was studying philosophy at Chapel Hill and sleeping in bunks and eating hot food at Parris Island and Camp Lejeune and Quantico, they had been living in foxholes praying to stay alive. Now I was going among them with bright new gold bars on my collar and nothing else. I had no Pacific theater ribbon, no battle stars, no purple heart. I had no natural right to command them, and they knew this as well as I did. I wanted to be back in the company office. I regretted every step that had brought me among them, but my epiphany came too late. I could not retreat. I went through their noise and knew that some of them were jeering. In their barracks room, their voices seemed to grow louder. I realized that I was all but helpless. I had nothing but my own demeanor and my own prudence—which should have kept me in my office—on which to rely.

Except for the noise, nothing happened. I'm sure that I was cursed, but the curses were indistinguishable, lost in the general shouting. The troops made way for me. I wasn't jostled. No one even touched me. I returned to my office, and as the night lengthened the shouting began to subside. The men had had their celebration, but they were marines after all. They respected themselves too much to start a riot. I remembered this night later when I was driving from Nashville to Washington, where I would be discharged. Still in uniform, I stopped on a Saturday night at a crossroads store in East Tennessee and came among a group of men drinking whiskey from shot glasses. They were pretty well in their cups, as the marines had been on VJ day, and one of them said, "Lieutenant, you're a son of a bitch."

I looked at this man whom I had never seen before in surprise, if not astonishment.

"I've always wanted to say that," the man said. "All the time I was in the army, I wanted to call every officer I saw a son of a bitch."

After the Japanese surrender, Chuck, a close friend with whom I had been stationed off and on since we left boot camp, got an automobile. Chuck's grandfather had founded a company, a greatly successful enterprise that his father and uncles now ran. His father owned a prewar Packard, an enormous car with leather upholstering and wood trim, with jump seats and a hood that seemed to stretch halfway to the horizon. It had a twelve-cylinder engine that appeared to be big enough to power a ship. It hadn't had much maintenance during the war. The brakes were not good, the engine missed now and then, and the tires, of a size that was no longer made, were badly worn. But it was an automobile, and I couldn't ride in it without being reminded of Al Capone. Once several of us got Thompson guns from the armory and long cigars from the PX and posed for photographs around the Packard hoping to look like gangsters, but in our uniforms we still looked like marines.

Like all branches of the service, the Marine Corps, which had grown to six divisions and numerous support personnel as the war advanced, now had to discharge tens of thousands. The federal government had established a point system to determine the order of discharge. Points were given for length of service, with double points for service overseas. Chuck and I had relatively few points. We would have to wait a while before we left the corps, but Washington, D.C., was a good place for waiting. We were ordered to Marine Barracks, and the Packard, which had come from Indiana to Lejeune on a flatbed truck, traveled in the same way to Washington. Chuck and I went a couple of days early to be on hand when the Packard arrived. We stayed in a hotel and didn't report to Marine Barracks until after dark on the day we were ordered to be there. As soon as we passed through the gate, Chuck, his eye quicker than mine, saw through an unshuttered window two female telephone operators who had removed their uniforms and were working the switchboard in their slips. Seeing a woman in her slip was nothing about which to get excited, but one of the girls was breathtakingly beautiful. Her name, as we found out later, was Barbara; her father Chinese, her mother Caucasian, she a gorgeous combination of the best elements of both strains.

It took a little while for us—I should say Chuck, because he had seen her first—to meet Barbara. For a week or two, there wasn't space for us in the BOQ. We rented a room in a big house on East Capitol

Street. We often had dinner at the post, and we drank and played bridge in one of the living rooms of the BOQ, but you had to get into the flow of life on the base to meet the women. Except for Betty, a lieutenant who was a stunning blonde counterpart to dark-haired Barbara, and who went out only with Dan, a handsome officer who later played for the Green Bay Packers, almost all the women were enlisted personnel who would not eat where we ate and not drink where we drank and who, under the letter of military law, we were not supposed to meet socially. At last, Chuck and I got rooms on the post where we could observe the habits of the women: when they might go to the PX, when they came to work, when they left, and where they lived, because there were few, if any, female quarters at Marine Barracks. Finally, we met Barbara and a few other girls with passable looks. Chuck and I double-dated in the Packard. My date and I occupied the wide backseat. Chuck and Barbara rode in the front. He might have been a more successful Lothario if he had allowed me to drive, or, even better, left me at home. When we parked, as we always did, the girls, if not the men, were conscious of the presence of each other.

For a few of his dates with Barbara, Chuck left me behind, but his success was no better. Barbara would allow him to go so far, but no farther. He was discouraged. Barbara was so attractive that he could not stop dating her, but he realized that his efforts were never going to succeed. He went out with other girls. Late one night, he and his date were on a couch in a living room of the BOQ. Romantic music came from a radio. All was going as well as he could have wanted. Then it was midnight, and the music stopped. The radio station was signing off. The announcer said they would close their broadcast day with a prayer. An Evangelical preacher warned against temptation and sin. The girl jerked upright on the couch. For Chuck, for that night at least, all was over.

Barbara continued to be prominent not only in Chuck's imagination but also in mine. She and I now worked in the same building. One day she came to my office and sat down on my desk, her beautiful legs not far below my eye level. Now, after sixty years, her image is vivid in my recollection. I remember the color of her stockings, her green skirt pulled above her knees. Maybe her face would not have launched a thousand ships, but, surely, her face and body together would have roused an armada. Chuck had seen her first. As long as he and I were together she would belong to him. My part was to suffer in silence, and I did.

I was in command of one department of the Marine Corps Schools that offered correspondence courses for those who had not finished high school or who wanted basic courses that might give them credit at some colleges. The department ran itself. My chief NCO had a Ph.D. in English; all my people were well educated. The courses were established. Protocols were in place. Chuck did various things. For a while, he was in charge of the brig, a job that suited him well. During one of our stints at Lejeune he urged that we do something to get ourselves incarcerated as a part of our Marine Corps experience, which I wouldn't have agreed to in any circumstances and certainly not at Lejeune, where the prisoners did hard time. As at most prisons, the yard was enclosed by a chain-link fence topped with razor wire. Every hour, night and day, the prisoners were required to leave their cells and run full speed across the yard to sit with their backs against the fence. Then they ran back to their cells to wait for the next command to run again. Chuck was interested in how the prisoners at Marine Barracks responded to their punishment. Once he took me into the brig to show me how some of those who were on bread and water ate only the soft inside of the loaf. Others ate only the crust.

Both of us served short stints at what President Roosevelt called Shangri-La, the presidential retreat in the Maryland mountains. A company of marines manned a perimeter to guard the premises whether or not the president was in residence. The officers lived in cabins that were small and sparsely furnished, and I had to share mine with a Doberman I had inherited from the officer before me or perhaps the one before him. This dog had once walked the perimeter, ready to attack anyone who came near except his handler. Having been detrained, he was now gentle and harmless, but he was as stubborn as a mule. In my cabin there was one easy chair, and he thought he ought to have it. I outweighed him, but not by as much as I would have liked. He was big and much faster than I. I would pull him out of the chair, but half of the time he could get back into it before I could sit down. When I finally got the chair away from him, he fooled me into believing that he had to go out, but when I got up to open the door, he occupied the chair.

The dog was the liveliest aspect of my life when I was in Maryland. There were two other officers stationed there, a captain and a first lieutenant. Both of them were from the South. The captain had been at Iwo Jima and, I think, was going to stay in the Marine Corps. The lieutenant, while not illiterate, didn't know how to pronounce many of the words that he saw in print. Our topics of conversation were limited. We had a movie every week, but, unlike films shown at larger bases, these were not new and the films themselves were in imperfect condition. The camp was a good place to read and to get caught up on your correspondence. I found a copy of Andrew Lytle's *The Long Night*, which I read with enjoyment and great admiration. Otherwise, the books were undistinguished. I was delighted to be ordered back to Marine Corps Schools after three weeks.

Washington was full of unattached women. Often at night, some of them were at the BOQ. With or without women present, we drank and now and then sang bawdy songs, and always, except during working hours and sometimes then, a bridge game—or more often two—was in progress. The executive officer at Marine Barracks was Major Lou Wilson, who later became commandant of the Marine Corps. He was the best officer I ever knew. He had won the Congressional Medal of Honor in one of the Pacific campaigns, and he had unbelievable command presence. Relations among the junior and junior field officers at Marine Barracks were largely informal, but nobody called Major Wilson "Lou," nor did he call any of us by our first names. He was tall and straight, and I never heard or heard of him raising his voice, but there was a tone of command in everything he said. He often played bridge at the BOQ at lunch; when his partner was a warrant officer whom he always addressed as Mr. McElroy, he was unbeatable. Both Major Wilson and Mac were from Mississippi. Mac had been on the verge of retirement when the Japanese attacked Pearl Harbor. He had been kept in the corps COG—convenience of the government. Now that he was going to be discharged, he was loath to go home.

"Lieutenant," he said, for he kept to the formal terms of address as punctiliously as did Major Wilson, "do you know what they do in Mississippi?"

"No, Mac. What?"

"They drink Coca-Cola and play Rook."

Mac liked to talk about the old Marine Corps when, in peacetime, everybody knew everybody else. According to Mac, in those days, to a great extent, the men governed themselves. Anybody suspected of stealing was put in coventry, which meant that nobody would speak to him or answer him when he spoke. Nobody would even ask him to pass the potatoes. If he asked that the potatoes be passed to him, no one would respond. The Marine Corps was so small that coventry would go with you wherever you went.

When the day came for Mac to be discharged, the adjutant, who had Mac's discharge papers, was on leave. Before he left, he asked me to tell Mac that his papers were on the dresser in the adjutant's room.

"Well, I can't go," Mac said.

I knew that his plans to depart the next day had all been made, but nothing could induce him to go into the adjutant's room. His instincts developed during his years in the old corps were too strong for him to risk being suspected of theft, even though he was going to be discharged. "I'll have to wait," Mac said, "until the lieutenant gets back."

I told him I would get the papers for him. "No, no, Lieutenant," he said, "I can't let you do that."

I went anyway, and Mac followed me. He stood in the doorway just outside the edge of the room and looked at me as I got the papers and brought them out. "I was watching all the time," Mac said. "If you have any trouble about this, call me."

I was eager to go home. I wanted to finish college, to go to graduate school, to try to be a writer. Before we could be discharged, we had to take what the government infelicitously called "terminal leave," the days we had accumulated during our service. I spent mine with Chuck on the boat his father brought down the inland waterway and across the Gulf of Mexico every fall to Fort Lauderdale. We got to Florida on military planes—with the navy to Norfolk, with the army to somewhere in North Florida, and, finally, on a general's personal plane, a refitted B-25, but without the general, to Miami. Chuck's mother, whose station wagon was shipped to Florida by rail every fall and, in the spring, sent back to Indiana, met us in Miami and took us to Lauderdale. The boat had two or three staterooms. Chuck and I shared one; his mother was in another.

There were two heads, a sizable salon, a small galley, and a spacious deck where Chuck's mother sometimes entertained friends for cocktails.

The people who regularly spent their winters at Fort Lauderdale seemed to form a small community, and they were all generous to Chuck and me. Some of them took us to dinner and invited us for drinks, asking us to join the group around the piano to sing well-known songs; they would gladly, I thought, have listened to our war stories, if we had had any to impose on them. Chuck's mother had lined up girls for us to date while we were there—twins, also from Indiana, who didn't re-motely resemble each other. This was a different society from that in which I had been raised. Certainly, like all human beings, these people must have had unfulfilled desires; they must have suffered losses and disappointments. Whatever these might have been, they were put aside. The women and the few men who were there sat under their rented cabanas and watched the waves break and glitter in the sun and talked contentedly to each other.

We visited Chuck's grandmother, who occupied a well-constructed house away from the beach, designed to be impervious to wind or water. A black couple who had worked for Chuck's family all their lives had come to Florida with Chuck's grandmother. The man, who had not gone to college, read Shakespeare and had memorized many passages from the plays, a talent about which Chuck's mother and his aunt had mixed feelings. They liked the couple well enough, but they complained to Chuck's grandmother that they were poor housekeepers; Chuck's mother wrote her name large in the dust on the baby grand piano. This was in vain. The grandmother liked her servants and declined to repri-mand them.

This was the last time that Chuck and I spent together. When our leaves ended, we started home and found that our luck as travelers had run out. No planes in Miami were scheduled to go near Washington. We got a lift with the navy to Jacksonville and loitered there for a couple of days hoping for a ride, but there was none available. We were running short of both time and money, so Chuck said that we would have to travel "steerage," and we caught buses to take us home. At the bus station, for the first time in our acquaintance, we seemed not to know quite what to say to each other. We made the usual farewell speeches: Good luck. Keep in touch. Around us, people, many of them in uniform, came and went. We shook hands. Chuck found his bus and went aboard. I caught my bus and, from a seat by a window, watched the Florida landscape. I slept a lot on the way home.

In Nashville I borrowed my mother's car and drove to Washington. The day that I had awaited eagerly for almost three years had arrived. I went through the required procedures and signed the papers that needed my signature. For some reason I felt that I was not quite ready to go. I stood in the middle of the parade ground and looked at the buildings. At one end was the house that the British had used as their army headquarters in the War of 1812, which was now home to the commandant of the Marine Corps. There were houses of other generals, the house of the colonel in command of the post, the BOQ where I had helped raise hell, the barracks that housed the enlisted men. There was the bell that was rung to mark the hours of the watch. One night, it had been the downfall of a drunk marine who had rung it for pleasure. Everything was in its place: the movie theater where the back rows were reserved for officers and where the marine band practiced and occasionally gave concerts; the sick bay where we had often gone to see the doctor, a navy lieutenant commander whom we called "Doc," looking for something to alleviate our hangovers; the brig that Chuck had briefly commanded. My car was packed. The gas tank was full. The road to Nashville and to the rest of my life lay ahead of me. Still, I hesitated. I continued to stand and look around, waiting, but not waiting either, for I expected nothing to happen, and nothing did. The April sun was bright on the flag that rippled in a slight breeze. The lines chimed against the metal flagpole.

After a moment more I got in and started my car. I drove through the gates and returned the sentry's salute. I was on my way home to Tennessee.

Chapter Eleven

Home Again

I came home to a new life, but not immediately. Eager to complete my college degree and to get on with my career, I enrolled in the spring quarter at Vanderbilt, but, as I should have known would be the case, it was not the Vanderbilt I had left. Only a few of those whom I had known before the war had returned in April 1946. Some had transferred to other universities, some had found jobs, some had turned into postwar hoboes bumming their way around the country, some rested at home until their government unemployment benefits ran out. Like me, the ones who did return had changed. I tried, halfheartedly, to resume life as a member of a fraternity. I reestablished connection with some of my old high school friends. I started dating Jean again, but our relationship was as stormy as ever. We parted, and for a while I dated a girl, a year or two older than I, whose husband had been killed in the war. At the same time I was making new friends at Vanderbilt, people who were interested in the things that interested me—literature, writing, philosophy. On most weekday mornings we had coffee together in the student center. We worked hard and were determined to play hard, and we became competent at both.

One afternoon, when I was reading in the browsing room of the library, Jane appeared and spoke to me—and what? It would be wrong to say that I fell in love at first sight. For one thing, it was not first sight. Both of us had entered Vanderbilt in the fall of 1941. We had had a class or two together, so I remembered her from that other time as a fellow student, but I didn't recall how beautiful she was or how bright. Not that afternoon, but soon, I asked her for a date. I went out with her as much as I could, and it didn't matter to me where we went or what we did as long as we were together; what I remember most fondly is being alone with her. Sometimes we took our bottle and drank in what passed for bars in those days of semiprohibition. We went to a pie wagon on West End Avenue, a very small eating place with a severely limited menu, where we listened to records on the jukebox and drank beer. We parked on the Vanderbilt campus and half listened to Larry Munson broadcast the play of the local baseball team. Being deeply in love, I thought about her all the time, and, when we couldn't be together, I phoned her and we talked for a long time.

We conducted our courtship amid a riotous group of friends. We were all reading the work of "lost generation" writers—Hemingway and Fitzgerald, Malcolm Cowley and E. E. Cummings—and we thought of ourselves as heirs to their angst, although that word had not yet come into common usage. We halfway knew that we were only pretending, playing a game that added gravity to our lives, which were really lived in happiness and all but invulnerable confidence. We had cookouts and picnics, drinking illegally in the public parks. Jane and I drove around town aimlessly, sitting close to each other on the bench-front seats of that day; if Jane was driving, she would likely go the wrong direction down a one-way street. One Saturday morning with our friends we rented a motel room in which we had an orange-blossom breakfast. All involved had vowed to eschew food and start the day with drinks made of orange juice and gin. Did we also include raw eggs? We probably did, but the gin prevailed, and by nine o'clock we were well on the way to being drunk with the rest of Saturday morning and all of Saturday afternoon and night still before us.

Ward Allen and Albert Smith were my two closest friends. Ward was small and fair. For most of his life, he has looked younger than he was. He is very bright, a diligent student of the classics as well as of English literature. He and I were in the same class at Vanderbilt, working our way toward the comprehensive examination in English and American literature that was required of all senior English majors. We studied together, exchanged ideas, read the same critics as well as the same primary texts. One afternoon Ward surprised me by saying that we need not be concerned with our test on the metaphysical poets. We could let T. S. Eliot take the exam for us—which we did, both of us parroting what Eliot had written. Albert Smith was younger than Jane and Ward and me. I don't quite remember how he came into our lives. He was a good actor and starred in several student productions, so I may have met him in the drama department, in which I took several courses. He was very bright and fun to be with, a good raconteur and a humorous observer of human folly, but I've wondered if his attachment to us might have contributed to some of the trials he endured later. For twenty years or so he was a practicing alcoholic; then he straightened himself out and became the publisher of several small newspapers in Kentucky. He had a full scholarship to Vanderbilt, but when Ward and I graduated, and Jane and I left to go to Iowa, he dropped out of school and went to New Orleans.

Between my graduation from Vanderbilt in June 1947 and our marriage and immediate departure for Iowa City in August, Jane and I passed a memorable summer, another period in my life of peace and joy. To circumvent price controls during the war, liquor dealers boxed a bottle of good whiskey with two or three bottles of bad rum and charged an exorbitant price for the package; the price of the rum, which had not been sold in the United States before the war, was not controlled. When the war ended, price controls were relaxed, more whiskey became available, and the dealers sold off their stocks of rum for a dollar a bottle. Did Jane and I really drink a bottle of rum a day? Surely not. Surely there were days when we read, days when she honed her thesis on Red Warren—she needed to write only a précis of it to get her M.A. But my principal memory of that wonderful summer is of a little place downtown, on Church Street, I think, where we sat in a booth and drank our rum and occasionally were visited by friends who seemed to know where to find us. I like to remember that time, unique to us, never to be reprised—just as it shouldn't have been.

Helen Ransom, daughter of John Crowe Ransom, was one of Jane's closest friends. When she and Jane were together, it seemed to me that the sum total of feminine pulchritude had gathered at one place. Helen had small features, a pageboy haircut, and dark eyes that often seemed wary, as if she was expecting the unexpected and wasn't sure that the unexpected would be fun. She was smart, but mercurial. When she failed to complete a paper for Donald Davidson, she used makeup to give herself a black eye, which doubtless did not deceive Mr. Davidson, as she must have known it wouldn't; but Mr. Davidson was an old friend of her father's, and, regardless of what he might have thought, he let the moment pass. Duane Foreman, as handsome as Helen was beautiful, had come to Vanderbilt from Mississippi, graduated at the top of his class in medical school, and interned at Johns Hopkins. He was in the army when he and Helen married in the chapel at Kenyon College— Jane was in the wedding—and in the summer of 1947 they were back in Nashville, where Duane was soon to start a residency in neurosurgery at Vanderbilt. Duane was an alcoholic, but at that time, when everyone we knew was drinking too much too often, he seemed no different from the rest of us in our determination to act out our romantic vision of how artists and writers and the enlightened in general ought to live.

I proposed to Jane one afternoon in the front seat of an automobile. I loved her very much, and she loved me; for the past few months we had spent every possible moment in each other's company. So I was surprised at how difficult it was for me to speak the words and how poorly I spoke them. Even now, except for the way I felt, the details of that moment are vague in my recollection. I think we were in her mother's car. I think she was driving on Broad Street. I think that in the weeks before I proposed I had assumed, without realizing it, that our engagement was already a fait accompli, but when she said yes, I was pleased beyond my expectations. We told our friends of the engagement. We—really Jane—made plans for the wedding. We received good wishes and congratulations; we went to parties; we waited for the wedding day and talked at length about what we would do with the rest of our lives.

The night of the wedding, August 30, 1947, we hid our automobile from friendly pranksters and were married by a Methodist preacher in the chapel at West End Methodist Church. This clergyman who married us—a well-meaning old gentleman—had insisted that he counsel us before the wedding, so we went to his apartment and heard him talk, but I don't remember a word he said. As good manners required, we thanked him, told him good night, kissed on the way to the car, and went on to have a beer or a drink or to park in a dark place and sit with our arms around each other. After the wedding reception, we rode away from Jane's house with Helen at the wheel. She was as wild a driver as Jane, but not nearly as skillful. We sped away, trying to elude our friends, and we had a thrilling ride. At the first corner, Helen missed the turn, bouncing on the curb and off again. At the next corner the tires squealed so loudly that even if our pursuers had lost sight of us, they would have been able to locate us again by the noise of Helen's driving. But she was intrepid in her recklessness. She took us on such a circuitous route that I began to fear she had become lost while trying to evade those who were chasing us. Finally, free from our friends, or sufficiently far away from them to escape, we got in our car, told Helen good-bye, and drove away. We spent the night in a hotel in Clarksville, spending the night together for the first time, and set out the next day for St. Louis, where we would stay for a brief honeymoon.

In those days, most automobiles were not air-conditioned, so on the morning after our wedding we rode north through Kentucky and Illinois with the windows open, the rush of air from outside making it difficult for us to talk. In the enforced silence, I considered how my life had changed from one day to the next. I felt a great sense of responsibility for Jane that I had not anticipated. I was so deeply in love throughout our courtship that there was no space left in my brain or my heart for considerations of what we would do in the future. Now I wondered whether I would provide her with whatever she would need. I wasn't sure. I had heard too many stories of writers, among them some of the very best, whose devotion to their art left their wives and their children to fend for themselves. I resolved never to do that. I didn't know how I would make a living as a writer, but I wanted very much to be a writer, and I was determined to take care of Jane. She sensed my mood. She put her hand on mine, and her touch restored my confidence. I told myself that all would be well. At St. Louis, we went to the zoo and watched elephants do their tricks. We ate at a good restaurant or two and drank at some bars where, not surprisingly, I drank too much. Then we went to Iowa City, to what for both of us was a new world.

Chapter Twelve

Carousing with People; Walking with Dogs

Under the terms of the "the GI Bill," an act of Congress giving benefits to veterans, anyone who had served in the military during World War II was eligible to receive from the federal government one day's education for each day served, with tuition paid, books furnished, and a monthly stipend of $75 or $90 a month depending on whether one was married. I had been awarded a teaching fellowship that paid me about as much as the government paid, and Jane's father had left her an insurance policy that would pay her $50 a month for the next two or three years, but we did desperately need a place to live. With the influx of discharged soldiers and sailors and marines, enrollment at the University of Iowa had grown from 10,000 to 30,000, and housing for married students was almost impossible to find. A few Quonset huts, relics of the war years, had been divided into apartments and were offered to new faculty—Andrew and Edna Lytle lived briefly in one—and to married students who had children. For the rest of us, no provision had been made, and none was promised. Jane and I stayed a few days in a cheap hotel, but it wasn't cheap enough for us to stay there long. In the company of many other married students, we waited every afternoon at the newspaper office, bought a copy of the paper as soon as it was published, consulted the want ads, and searched for a place to rent. The first we found was with Lester and Vernell Norton. She taught Latin, perhaps at the university, but, if so, her appointment was temporary, made because of the sudden increase of students. Lester was a self-professed jack-of-all-trades, and he was working to complete the house where he and Vernell and, for a week or so, Jane and I lived. But house is not right; there were two houses. The one in which we lived had been moved from somewhere else and placed next to the other. Lester had joined the two, with what was planned as an entry, but it was unfinished and remained so long after Jane and I had moved.

Lester worked. He rose early to saw and hammer, to join one pipe to another, to hang a side of drywall, to paint. Every day, he worked on a different part of the house—a bedroom, the living room, the front steps. He mixed and poured concrete for steps, but when he failed to complete them in a day, he turned his attention to another project, leaving the half-empty forms to darken and warp in the weather. In our kitchen to be, we had a hot plate, maybe two, on which to cook, perhaps an icebox, but certainly no refrigerator. There was running water, but not in the house. Vernell had a large bottle that she filled from the outside spigot and kept in her kitchen, which also had a stove and pots and pans and dishes, a can opener, a measuring cup, and, insofar as I could tell, most of the accoutrements of an ordinary kitchen. We would have liked to have a real kitchen and closets in which to hang our clothes and more than the few chairs and the bed with which our side of the house was furnished. But, most of all, we wanted the bathroom that Lester had promised us. He had shown us the fixtures already purchased before we moved in, but the fixtures remained in their crates. While Lester flitted from one task to another, like a butterfly turned carpenter, we and he and Vernell used a privy that stood slightly off balance at a discreet distance behind the house. The final crisis in our lives with Lester came when Jane awoke one morning to find two rats fighting by the bed, not far from her hand. She screamed, more in anger than in fear; inspired by this confrontation, she found for us a basement apartment in a house in town. It was tawdry and damp. We had an ancient foldout couch to sleep on. To reach the shower or the commode, which were in separate compartments, we had to walk past the coal bin, but this was better than walking across the backyard, regardless of the weather.

We had no phone. If we got permission, we could use the landlord's phone, but he and his wife and even their teenage daughter were strait-laced people who never fully trusted Jane and me. One night, or morning, because it was after twelve, the landlord knocked on our door. I was wanted on the phone. Who would call at that hour except in a case of emergency? Was it long-distance? Were we to hear bad news from Nashville? Our landlord, his wife, and his daughter must have been as curious as Jane and I were; they stood two steps from the telephone, waiting, I suppose, to see what would transpire. The call was from the Jefferson Hotel, not more than a mile or two from our apartment. The caller was Cal Lowell. I had not seen him or been in touch with him since Easter weekend, 1943, when he and Jean Stafford were living with Allen and Caroline Tate. I was surprised that Cal remembered me, more surprised that he knew I was in Iowa, and even more surprised that he had found somebody—most likely Paul Engle, the director of the Writers' Workshop—who knew how we could be reached. He even knew that I was married, and he invited Jane and me to come to his room. He was lonely. Would we come?

To me, Cal always looked a little scruffier than I remembered from the last time I saw him, which may have been a part of his charm. His strong, square jaw was balanced by the spectacles that seemed to drift up and down his nose. If he was wearing a coat, the collar pulled toward the right or the left as if it was tight on one shoulder and loose on the other. That night he wasn't wearing a coat. His shirt was wrinkled; his tie was halfway knotted; his hair, always somewhat disorderly, needed combing. I went to the hotel with some trepidation. Cal was not only enormously talented; he was enormously learned. When he and Peter Taylor and Randall Jarrell were living in the same house at Kenyon, and John Crowe Ransom could choose among them for someone with whom to converse, he always chose Cal. I feared that I wouldn't be able to sustain my end of the conversation with him, but that night Cal did all the talking.

Cal told us that, not long before he came to Iowa City, he had gone to St. Elizabeths Hospital in Washington to visit Ezra Pound, whom the federal authorities has decided to treat as a madman rather than as a traitor. Cal said that Pound was quite sane except when he was discussing economics, on which subject he was quite crazy. There was irony here. Pound had said that William Butler Yeats was sane except on the subject of mysticism. Perhaps in talking to Cal there were subjects that were best avoided, but that night he talked only of literature, and he talked well. He discussed Pound's work. He appeared fully to understand the *Cantos,* but I didn't understand them, and I can't remember what he said. Later he spoke of *The Canterbury Tales,* which he knew even better than he knew the *Cantos.* He told the stories. He commented on the verse. Turning to the Romantics, he said very good things of Keats, and somewhat to my disdain, for I held firmly to my youthful prejudices then, he spoke a kind word or two about Shelley. Did he see in my expression that I demurred? I know I didn't respond, that I had no opportunity to express my views, which was no doubt just as well, but at this moment Cal said something that Jane and I have remembered and occasionally quoted to each other over the ensuing years. "So few people," Cal said, "do anything well."

His reading the next night was controlled, his comments on his poems clear and informative, but he hadn't slept since he arrived in Iowa City. After his reading, he went to a reception at Paul Engle's house and then stayed up and talked to students when the reception was over. His voice grew louder. He began to address any stranger who would listen to him. As soon as he could the next day, Paul put Cal on a plane to Chicago, where he was met by an astonished Allen Tate. Physically, Allen and Cal were a strange pair. Allen was old enough to be Cal's father. He was short and slightly built and already stricken with symptoms of the emphysema that ultimately would take his life. Cal was big, burly, and very strong. When Cal stood on a table in a Chicago restaurant to harangue the other diners, Allen persuaded Cal to go to Bloomington, Indiana, where Peter Taylor met his plane. Seeing how much Cal needed help, Peter put Cal on a plane for Boston, where he entered a sanitarium.

In many ways, Iowa was foreign to Jane and me. We moved from the basement apartment to a house and from the house to an upstairs apartment where we were treated well by our landlord and his wife, but the manners of the people in Iowa City were not our manners, and I'm sure that they found our way of doing things strange as well. We made friends with other graduate students and their wives and husbands. Some were already illustrious. Robie Macauley was above most of us. Most of us who had fellowships taught one of the "core courses" in literature that were required of all freshman. Robie taught a course in the Russian novel that was open to more advanced undergraduates. Tony Hecht was already writing publishable poetry, some of which I read in manuscript when Tony and I had coffee together. Robie introduced Jane and me to Flannery O'Connor.

Flannery was the rising star in the fiction workshop, but unlike Cal Lowell, who looked like a poet, Flannery's appearance disguised her wit and her brilliance. She had dull blonde hair, a round face, legs as straight as sticks, and, the night that Robie brought her to see us, she wore no jewelry. She spoke with a heavy southern accent that she would never lose in spite of her years at Iowa and later in New York and New England. Her appearance and the sound of her voice were aspects of her self-assurance. She could, Jane thought, have made herself less plain by paying more attention to her makeup and her hair, but she didn't need to be beautiful. She knew who she was—a descendent of one of the oldest Catholic families in Georgia and one of the few writers of her time with an original voice. Her eye for detail and her ear for dialogue were so good that occasionally a speech or a descriptive phrase would briefly divert the reader from the main thrust of the story. That night she told us—a tale that would become famous—of being dressed by her mother in a snowsuit, a superfluous anomaly in South Georgia, to be photographed by a newsreel cameraman who had come to take pictures of her chicken, which could walk backward—and did, disappearing in an oleander bush before the cameraman could get a proper shot of it. She laughed at everybody, including herself, but she took her religion seriously. Although she seldom spoke of it, the sense of it was a part of her being. It informed her life and shaped her fiction.

The list of students in the workshop who would later earn distinction was long, but not all who were enrolled were on it. Others were memorable for other things. We knew a couple from California—Ted and his wife, Mike—who came from rich families and who had arrived with an ancient bulldog named Roddy who was so productively flatulent that humans could hardly stand to be around him. Ted's and Mike's parents sent them boxes of gourmet food—olives stuffed with anchovies and specially prepared hams and exotic cheeses. They could afford Jack Daniel's and Dewar's and Courvoisier, and they distributed it generously, but to eat the food and drink the booze you had to go to their apartment and expose yourself to the unpleasant presence of the bulldog. Sometimes they shut the dog in another room, but somebody always forgot and opened the door, and the old dog would return and plop down on the floor and resume his deplorable habit.

Good or bad, promising or pedestrian, we gathered at one another's apartments and drank as if we were geniuses. Looking back from my prudent old age, I wonder that we all survived. Sufficiently inebriated to need fresh air, we sometimes took walks on winter nights, neglecting to wear coats or gloves, although the temperature was often below freezing. In my memory, we were constantly engaged in arguments—about literature, of course, sometimes about books such as *Finnegans Wake,* which none of us had read in its entirety. We took issue with each other's politics. Sometimes our very manners were in conflict. Late one night, Ted, weary of our wrangling, left his living room and returned carrying an enormous revolver, a Colt .44 with bullets plainly visible in the cylinder, and ordered us to stop our argument. It would be wrong to say that the rest of us were suddenly rendered sober, but we were possessed by prudence. We stopped talking, but it seemed to me that silence was not what the moment required.

"Well, of course," I said, "you're right. We shouldn't have been fussing at each other."

I apologized, but it was hard to think of anything else to say, and the silence that seemed by its nature dangerous fell once more. But women, and southern women best of all, can talk on almost any occasion, and talk prettily when the situation warrants. So Jane talked, and talked prettily, about what I don't remember. Soon, we were sufficiently calmed by her soothing voice to say good night to Ted and make our getaway.

On another night when we had been at someone else's house drinking our usual brands of cheap whiskey, Jane and I achieved what I would have thought impossible in a town the size of Iowa City: we got lost. Although we had lived in Iowa City for more than a year, the familiar streets seemed suddenly strange to me. There was no other traffic; no lights burned in houses or in stores. The streetlights seemed themselves to move as I drove past them. After I had driven for a while, Jane and I realized that we were in strange territory, going down a road that we had never seen before, passing signs that directed us to places we had never been. The road on which we drove began to narrow. We looked for a place to turn around and did not find one. We came to a one-lane bridge, crossed it, and stopped in a field of corn that was taller then our automobile.

Where were we? Where had we been? Where were we going? For that moment, we were the quintessential lost souls of our time, our very identity a mystery. I put the car in reverse and backed tentatively into the field, the wheels dropping slightly as they left the road, cornstalks slapping the car as loud as pistol shots. For a moment, I was afraid to try to go forward. If our wheels spun in the loose ground, we would have to spend the night in our car. In the morning, we would likely be discovered by a farmer who would not approve of our bohemian antics. Finally, I put the car in gear and pressed the accelerator with the lightest touch I could accomplish. The wheels spun, but we moved, slowly onto the road, slowly back toward the bridge, slowly retracing our route, which we were relieved to remember. Jane, ever heroic, seemed to take this adventure in stride. Speaking in the most amiable terms, she helped me find our way home, to our own apartment, to our own bed, to the misery we, or at least I, would feel the next morning.

Our lives were not always riotous in Iowa. In order to receive my student stipend from the government, I took courses in the summer when the heat rose as ferociously as the cold of winter. Because our un-air-conditioned apartment usually cooled as night fell, we slept, or tried to sleep, in the daytime and stayed up all night. I worked in a cor- ner of the bedroom, trying to write the stories that would compose my thesis and the papers that my summer seminar required. At midnight, we walked. We left our apartment, stuffy and redolent from the cigarettes I smoked, and moved through the semidarkness of a quiet and peaceful world. Sometimes we held hands. Sometimes we talked. But, in conver- sation or in silence, we felt very happy to be with each other, happy to be where we were, doing what we did. But in Iowa City at midnight, not all things slept.

One night at a corner of our usual route, a dog, its breed and color unidentifiable in the poor light, joined us. He—or she—stayed with us until we got back to our door. The next night, the same dog was waiting for us. Soon, there were other companions, dogs of various shapes and pedigrees, that waited in the same places every night to join our pro- cession. At first there were two or three. Finally there were half a dozen or more, nice dogs that created no disturbance. Remembering the soft-ness of the nights, the comportment of the dogs, the closeness that Jane and I felt, it is hard not to think of those midnight walks as our imper-fect version of a peaceable kingdom. Sometimes, the only sound was that of the dogs' footsteps. They never barked, not at each other, not at anything we passed or at anything they might have heard. They went with us to our doorstep as if they were seeing us safely home.

I didn't realize then that as a writer I had reached my beginning at the end of the southern literary renaissance. Like most people growing up in Nashville in the 1930s, I knew a lot about the Civil War and about the Confederate defeat that was generally deplored but not fully ac-knowledged. My grandmother's memory was filled with the stories her father had told about the siege of Vicksburg, and she passed them on to me. He did not die until the year I was born, so my mother and aunts and uncle also remembered him, and they, too, had heard him talk about the war. In his heart, he had never surrendered. He didn't like Yankees, and he recalled the agony he had felt, the regret that transcended a sim-ple sense of guilt, when he took his first bites of Yankee food after Gen-eral Pemberton had surrendered and the blockade had been lifted. In the public schools that I attended, Robert E. Lee's picture hung in most rooms, and we were told a good deal about him and about the Confed-eracy, usually not in courses of formal study, but peripherally from the tales the teachers told and the books they read to us.

My mother recognized the deep ambiguity that informed our south-ern heritage. I was never told that slavery had been acceptable, and my mother and other members of my family saw and deplored the many wrongs that were inflicted on black people. She told me more than once of being on a bus when the driver ordered a black boy, a child, to take a seat in the rear, and the boy didn't understand what was happening to him. This must have been his first ride on a bus alone, and apparently he had never been coached on the terms of segregation. He was too young to dissemble. He was truly mystified and clearly hurt when the driver explained to him that he had to sit in the rear of the bus because he was a Negro. My mother sympathized with the boy, but if she thought that segregation on the bus was wrong and ought to be discontinued, she never said so. The knowledge of the failure of abolition as it was practiced in 1865 when the ex-slaves were turned out to fend for themselves with no education, no training beyond that of working in the fields to help them support themselves, made her wary of easy solutions.

So I was conscious of my own southernness and at least partially conscious of what that implied when, in the fall of 1941, I entered Vanderbilt, which at that time was a southern institution. Almost all the students were from Tennessee and contiguous states: Kentucky, Mississippi, Alabama, Georgia, Arkansas. As happened on many southern campuses, the Kappa Alpha fraternity held a Confederate ball every year on Robert E. Lee's birthday. Some of the members, dressed in Confederate uniforms, went on horseback to sorority houses to ask girls for dates and to deliver invitations. The Vanderbilt English department, perhaps the whole university, celebrated the Fugitives and the Agrarians, most of whom were still alive, and none of whom had yet fully rejected his southern heritage. I had a course under Frank Owsley, a historian who had contributed to *I'll Take My Stand* and who remained deeply unreconstructed. In my sophomore year, Donald Davidson led me to read southern writers: Faulkner, of course, and Robert Penn Warren, Andrew Lytle, Caroline Gordon, Stark Young, Roark Bradford, and others whose work fulfilled Mr. Davidson's standards for traditional southern literature. He deplored the work of T. S. Stribling as well as that of Erskine Caldwell, whom he seldom mentioned.

The writers whose work Mr. Davidson recommended set good examples, and I learned much about the craft of fiction from reading them and hearing Mr. Davidson discuss their books. But I didn't realize then, and for a long time thereafter, that their world was not my world; their culture was almost foreign to me. Throughout the early years of my career, I worked in violation of the first rule of fiction or any other kind of writing: write about what you know. In *Sojourn of a Stranger*, my first novel, I finessed my ignorance by going back a hundred years to the time of the Civil War. I had to research the same details my literary forebears had researched when they wrote historical fiction, and, like mine, their efforts to transform events learned from history into the fabric of fiction were not always successful. Some of the political speeches and the medieval games played at the picnic in Allen Tate's *The Fathers* are not fully realized dramatically, and the same is true of some of the campfire and war scenes in Andrew Lytle's *The Long Night*. The difficulty of writing traditional historical fiction in the twentieth and now the twenty-first century is compounded by the speed with which the details of life change, and by the fragmentation of cultural and ethical values.

My second novel, *The Long, Long Love,* was better than *Sojourn of a Stranger,* and if I had been constant in applying the lessons I learned from it, I think I would have written more and better books. In *The Long, Long Love,* I was able to take an ironic view of the Old South and the Civil War and show the folly of worshipping the past, but when I considered the subject of my next novel, I turned again to the past, which was a mistake I should not have made, and one that I had difficulty rectifying. My contemporaries among southern writers sometimes attempt to involve William Faulkner in their own failures. He was, some of us said, "a lion in the path," the genius who had used up our material and left us with only the dregs of our culture about which to write. Even so, his example should have been a warning to all southern writers of my generation: the South would be useful to writers of fiction as long as it remained a discrete culture, but southern writers would have to find new dramatic tensions and new themes to keep their books from being fragile imitations of what had gone before. Flannery O'Connor, perhaps alone among writers of her time, wrote original fiction by imposing acts of transcendent violence on her unmistakably southern characters and on the milieu in which they lived.

All of this, I learned later. At Iowa I tried to write about the traditional South and was rewarded with good grades for doing so. The fifty people who were members of the advanced fiction workshop met together once a week; one of us would read a story, and the others would criticize it. Each of us had an adviser with whom we met privately to discuss our manuscripts. My first adviser was Hansford Martin—known as "Mike"—whom I had known and with whom I had caroused at Chapel Hill. Mike had failed the army physical examination and avoided the draft during the war. Since we had been at North Carolina, he had published a novel, and he was a pretty good teacher of fiction writing. He was particularly adept at discovering points in my stories where I had fallen into generalities in order to spare myself the hard work of telling the fictional truth. We met in his office and in the bar of the Jefferson Hotel and in Jane's and my living room, where Jane listened and could have told us much if we had had sense enough to ask her. She was my best critic, the first one to let me read my work to her, the one I always trusted most.

Later, I worked under Andrew Lytle, whom Jane and I met for the first time in Iowa City. He came to see us one afternoon soon after his arrival, feeling more alienated than we. The living quarters he had been promised were in one of the remodeled Quonset huts that had been recently flooded, but not properly cleaned. When Andrew arrived with his family, furniture was stacked in the middle of the living room; there was a dirty streak on the walls that showed how high the water had risen; there was mud on the floor, and the rooms smelled of dampness and mold. Andrew told Jane and me that his daughters, Pamela and Kate, began to cry when they entered the hut. Then Edna began to cry. Seeing them cry, Andrew cried too, but perhaps more from anger than from disappointment. Andrew was ready to return to Tennessee, but he had come to take Paul Engle's place while Paul was on leave, so Paul rented his house to Andrew, an arrangement that was doomed to fail.

Paul and Andrew were as different temperamentally as the cultures whence they came. Paul seemed rude, sometimes devoid of manners. When he decided a party at his house had endured long enough, he said so and herded his guests out the door. He was a notorious womanizer, and a couple of times when Jane and I were going home for holidays, Paul borrowed our apartment for his assignations, saying that he needed a quiet place to work. Except for his children, two beautiful little girls whom he adored, Paul's major devotion was to the workshop. He seemed to be free of the jealousy that often exists among writers. He brought to Iowa poets and novelists whose writing was better known and more highly respected than his. They read from their work and criticized our efforts in meetings of the workshop and drank with the workshop faculty and the graduate students at Paul's house and often somewhere else when Paul's party ended. Some of them stayed in Iowa City for a week or longer, undoubtedly testing Paul's patience and his stamina, but I never heard him complain.

After Andrew moved into Paul's house, he became more comfortable in Iowa City. He was a good teacher. Donald Davidson had taught me how to use physical details. Now Andrew began to teach me how to select only the best, most effective details, which, if done with skill, would tighten the prose and move the narrative forward. At one of my sessions with Andrew we spent the hour talking about one scene: a boy going into a drugstore. From time to time, Andrew strayed from the topic. He had a lot of eclectic knowledge, little facts that were interesting but not always true. Once, he told me that an old Jewish custom freed the groom from any work for the first year of his marriage. I was later told by the daughter of a rabbi that this wasn't true, but at the time I assumed it was. Being myself newly married, I recognized Andrew's telling me this as a reprimand, but one that I didn't fully understand. Did he mean that I should stop trying to write until I became better accustomed to being married? Was he suggesting only that I ought to work harder? I was afraid to ask.

Andrew and Paul, wary of each other from the beginning of their acquaintance, fell out about a broken storm window at Paul's house. Andrew, who had moved to other quarters, was enraged that Paul would think he had broken a window or anything else and not offered to pay for it. Paul might have thought that Andrew's failure to pay was an over-sight. They spoke the same language, but the ways they spoke it—the nuances of phrase, even the meanings of some words—were different. Decades later, one of the reasons for Andrew's break with Allen Tate, whom he had called "brother" and known for half a century, was a con-frontation between Andrew and Allen's wife, Helen, she from Minne-sota and as untutored as Paul had been in the southern conventions by which Andrew lived. He had called at Allen's house, he said later, and Helen had spoken to him "through the screen." What Andrew and Paul said to each other or whether Paul spoke to Andrew through the screen, a gesture the meaning of which would probably have been lost on Paul, Andrew never told me. But his insistence on the importance of his own deportment and his interpretation of the behavior of others helped confirm me in my own southernness. I should have known better. What came naturally to Andrew did not come naturally to me.

Our allegiance to the South and to southern ways increased after Jane and I induced Ward Allen to come to Iowa City. At our suggestion, Ward had applied unsuccessfully for a teaching assistant's job at the uni-versity. I suppose that when the three of us went out together the night before we left Nashville to return to Iowa, we all thought we wouldn't be together again until our Christmas vacation. Late in the evening, when we all had had a few drinks, Jane and I insisted that Ward come with us to Iowa City. He could find something to do, and we needed his company. He agreed. We set a time for us to pick him up the next morning, and when we got to his mother's house on Ashwood Avenue, he waited at the curb, suitcase at his side. The next day, as I was registering for the fall semester, Seymour Pitcher, who was in charge of the core courses in literature, asked me if I knew Ward Allen. Since he had written Ward late in the summer, a teaching assistant's job had become available. Professor Pitcher wondered if I thought Ward was still interested in the position and how long it would take Ward to get to Iowa City. Not long, I assured him, and an hour later Ward had been hired.

Ward rented a room in a house not far from us. He charmed his landlady, whose goodwill he would need before he returned to Nashville, made friends with the other roomers, and bought an old pump organ, elaborately carved and still workable though of dubious pitch and deplorable tone, on which he learned to play familiar hymns. Then he bought, or perhaps simply adopted, a small black puppy of no particular breed that was energetic and friendly but not housebroken and whom he named after the obscure poet Nahum Tate, who had rewritten Shakespeare's plays in order to give the tragedies happy endings. Ward seemed to take Nahum Tate—he was always referred to by his full name—and his bad deportment as a matter of course. He taught his classes, he played his organ, and the dog, when not more dubiously engaged, cavorted around the room or slept near Ward's feet perfectly contented. We went with Ward to auction sales, where he bought antique furniture to send home to his mother, who was an antiques dealer. He went with us to parties where sooner or later our devotion to the South became a topic of conversation and then of argument. For all of us, our alienation from the North and from the modern world was compounded. I think that in our studied southernness, we must have been insufferable. In extenuation, I can only plead youth and ignorance.

In the national election of 1948, Henry Wallace, who had been vice president to Franklin Roosevelt from 1940 to 1944, had broken with the Democrats and was running as the presidential candidate of the

Progressive Party. Seymour Pitcher, who had given Ward a job, was the Progressive Party candidate for senator, and for reasons that I never discovered he thought that Jane and I were liberals. English professors at Iowa, in addition to Paul Engle, often entertained graduate students. Austin Warren, whose wife had recently died, entertained groups of us with his profound and often lively conversation and with performances on the small organ that was installed in his living room, a considerably later model than the one Ward had bought at auction. Sometimes Jane and I were invited to Professor Pitcher's house, and when he became a candidate our invitations increased. He thought of us as rare birds: liberals from the benighted South, and he introduced us as such—most memorably when Glen Taylor, Wallace's vice presidential candidate, came to Iowa City. "These are the people from Tennessee," Professor Pitcher said, "the ones I was telling you about."

This was the stuff of comedy, but Jane and I dared not laugh. We had no idea how the deception we were living had begun, but apparently it had gone on too long for us to correct it. We greeted Taylor—who was traveling in a station wagon and looked a little worn—with all the enthusiasm we could muster. A proper script for this encounter would have had us give ourselves away to the humorous outrage of all who were present. But it wouldn't have done. Professor Pitcher was a gentle man whom, without meaning to, I had deceived. So Jane and I made our polite responses, and we left the reception feeling a little sheepish.

Mr. Pitcher also entertained John Crowe Ransom when he came to Iowa to lecture. In the afternoon, Mr. Ransom had talked about prosody, and to the amazement of most of us—and I think to the outrage of some of the graduate students and younger faculty—he had illustrated his discussion with nursery rhymes. He wrote on the blackboard, "Sing a song of sixpence," and, as he wrote, he recited the poem in his wonderful Tennessee-Oxford accent. Mr. Ransom was a man of great self-control. Like Red Warren, he didn't reveal much about his inmost thoughts except when he was discussing literature, and even then he seemed to be perfectly composed. That night at Mr. Pitcher's, a group of professors pulled their chairs into a circle around Mr. Ransom as if to prevent his escape and began to question him, sharply I thought, about the New Criticism. The questions were adversarial, and it appeared to Jane and me as if the questioners had planned in advance to take Mr.

Ransom to task for the lack of political and social engagement in both his criticism and his poetry. They never penetrated his even temper. His voice never rose in volume, never lost its amiable tone. The men who surrounded him claimed that his work was "inorganic." Smiling, but firm, Mr. Ransom denied the accusation. At the end of the evening, Mr. Ransom remained unruffled and polite. He said a pleasant good night to all who were present.

Whatever faults Paul Engle might have had as a writer and a husband, he was a faithful friend to me, and his devotion to the workshop transcended his own self-interest. He tried to hire Allen Tate to teach at Iowa, offering to pay Allen more than he, himself, was making. He brought to Iowa City every writer who would agree to come. Besides Cal Lowell and Red Warren and Mr. Ransom, Peter Taylor came, and, to my surprise, charmed some of the members of a class I taught with his southern accent. Stephen Spender came, and went to parties and drank all night with some of the students. William Empson, whose *Seven Types of Ambiguity* had made him famous in the literary world, paced the stage in the Old Capitol building spinning a book of paper matches on a straightened paper clip and holding his beard in front of his mouth and speaking through it. Ruthven Todd came from Scotland. W. H. Auden came after Jane and I had left, as did Dylan Thomas. The workshop developed its own momentum. Writers visited to lecture and read because of the reputation of the program as much as for the money they were paid, which was not as much, I think, as they received from other universities.

One night in the summer of 1948, Paul invited Jane and me to Stone City, his place in the country. He had some land and a stone house, old and commodious and substantial. The privy, no longer in use, but a feature of the property, was also built of stone. Like the house, its dimensions were generous, and Grant Wood, dead now, but famous not only in Iowa but throughout the country, had decorated the privy walls with murals. When Jane and I arrived that night, Mary and the children were away, and we found only Paul and a poet from Finland. The day had been very hot, and darkness brought no relief. The large rooms and high ceilings of the house helped lower the temperature, but not much. The windows were small. The walls and seams of the house were tight. Stone City, like most structures in the Iowa countryside, had been designed not to remain cool in the summer but to keep out the cold of winter. Besides the poet, Jane and I were the only guests, and communication was difficult. The poet knew no English. Jane and I were equally ignorant of Finnish. Both Paul and the poet spoke German, but neither of them seemed to be totally comfortable doing so. Paul offered us a drink and with it some disappointing news. There was no water. We had only straight gin to refresh us on that warm evening. The poet read to us from his work, but neither Paul nor we understood him. Paul topped off our glasses and urged the poet to read again. The poet complied, uttering syllables that sounded harsh to Jane and me and signified nothing.

I don't know how long we sat at the table in Paul's kitchen. In the absence of our understanding each other, there appeared to be nothing to do but drink, and with every sip we grew hotter and our thirst increased. How long do we have to do this? I wondered. How long must we stay? Jane asked herself. We thought that Paul must have wanted us at his house, or he wouldn't have invited us. Our presence brought to the gathering not much more than two very warm bodies. We tried to appear interested in the poetry. We tried to look serious or sad to reflect the emotion that we thought we saw in the poet's face. Once more, we saw the humor of the scene only later, what a crazy time that was, how funny our predicament would have been if we had watched other characters endure it while we ourselves were comfortably situated, neither thirsty nor hot. This evening survives in my memory as an image of our lives in Iowa. The heat of the night that a few months before or after would have been the sub-zero cold of winter; the house, ugly, but built to withstand all storms; the poet, whom we could not understand and who could not understand us. Except when he and Paul spoke German, we sat in isolation from each other, an isolation that Jane and I had often felt while we were in Iowa City. I still sometimes wonder why Paul invited us. But the invitation is a part of the image too: his rough hospitality; his careless generosity; his devotion to writing that extended to poetry or fiction written in languages that he did not understand.

Chapter Thirteen

Back Where I Longed to Be

I received my M.F.A. from the University of Iowa in June 1948, but teaching jobs, particularly for those without Ph.D.s, were difficult to find, and I had not found one. Baldwin Maxwell, head of the English department at Iowa, agreed that I could stay on for another year, teaching some required courses and making enough money to pay the rent and put food on the table and maybe buy a little whiskey if Jane and I handled our finances carefully, but this was not a real job, and at the end of the year I would once more be without employment. Then a kind Providence gave me a job at Vanderbilt. In the middle of the summer, Hudson Long, a professor of American literature at Vanderbilt, left to teach at Baylor, and Walter Clyde Curry, head of the Vanderbilt English department, hired me. I would teach twelve hours, four sections of freshman English in the first quarter, three sections of freshman English and one class in advanced composition in the second and third terms. I would receive, as Dr. Curry put it, "$3,000 for the nine months." The job was for one year only, although, Dr. Curry said, there was a "bare possibility" that something further would turn up. So Jane and I rejoiced and packed our bags and went to Nashville.

We rented one side of a duplex in a small subdivision of duplexes where many of our neighbors were friends or classmates, mostly men who had been to the war and the women who had married them. The neighborhood grew. Women had babies. We watched them carry their large stomachs up and down the street, getting the exercise that their doctors had ordered. Then the babies came and the women pushed them in carriages along the sidewalks. They talked to one another and admired each other's babies and fended off the friendly but often mischievous dogs who were intrigued by the new smells that had been introduced into their world and wanted to see what was in the baby carriages. Briefly this was a peaceful time. The war was over. The Korean conflict had not yet begun. But it did begin soon, and it went badly, and, along with the other services, the marines began to call up their reserves.

The active reserves, those who trained on weekends and for two weeks during the summer, were called first. Many members of the inactive reserve were called also. Their orders arrived through the mail, as mine would if I got them. Jane and I spent an anxious summer in 1951, waiting for the postman, who came twice a day then, and breathing daily sighs of relief when no orders arrived. Jane was pregnant, due to deliver her baby toward the end of June. I didn't want to leave her or the baby she was going to have, and I knew that even if I was allowed to stay in the United States, wherever I was stationed housing would be hard to find, and not very satisfactory if we could find it. We walked a lot at night before the baby was born, holding hands along the dark sidewalk, relieved that my orders had not come, anxious that they might come tomorrow. Then Pam was born, and like most fathers I was incompetent and of scant help, but when Jane got up to feed the baby in the early light of day, I got up with her and read to her in this quiet hour when all the rest of the world seemed to be asleep.

I assume that because my last duty in the marines was at Marine Corps Schools, and there was not much need of educators in Korea, I was never ordered to active duty. Vanderbilt hired me for another year. And I went to work on the novel that I hoped would secure my future at Vanderbilt when and if it was published. The idea for the novel had been suggested by Ward Allen, who told me what he knew about General James Winchester, who had brought his family from Maryland to Tennessee late in the eighteenth century. He brought some craftsmen with him and built a house in Sumner County, where he made friends with Andrew Jackson and John Overton, who, like Jackson, was rich and politically powerful. General Winchester farmed, speculated in land, joined with Jackson and Overton to found the city of Memphis, and made a lot of money. His son, Marcus Winchester, married an accomplished and beautiful octoroon whom he met in New Orleans, and they had a son who, as I imagined him, became the hero of my novel. So far, so good. All I knew about Marcus Winchester's son was that he had been born. Perhaps with hard work and ingenuity I could have found out more about him, but the point for me was not to know: instead, I needed to have a situation, a character with a problem who, if I could make him angular and complex and believable as a human being, would develop a story that I would not so much tell as follow.

I named my character Allen Hendrick. I gave him a father and mother and grandfather modeled on the characters described above; later I gave him a girl with whom to fall in love, and the girl's father and brother, who would refuse her permission to marry him. Did I know all this when I began? I don't know. Now, after fifty years, I don't remember. I did know that the Civil War would intervene in Allen's life, as it had truly intervened in the lives of all southerners who lived through it. I read a lot about the Civil War. I didn't know what I needed to know, but I knew that I needed to know more than I would put into my story. When Red Warren went to New Haven to begin teaching at Yale, someone asked him if, having left the South, he would start writing about New England. "God, no," Red replied. "I don't even know what the people outside New Haven eat for breakfast." He was making the same point that Hemingway made when he said that what the writer has to know is like the hidden part of an iceberg. The four-fifths that are underwater represent the details that are necessary knowledge for the writer but that never get into the story. As much as possible I had to feel the time and place, know it as profoundly as I could. So I read, maybe too much, because reading is much easier than writing.

I wrote at night. Teaching four sections of freshman English—a better teaching load than many others at other institutions struggled under at that time—meant that I had to grade four sets of themes a week, marking the errors and judging the content of one hundred papers. I taught and kept office hours in the morning. I graded papers and prepared for the next day's classes in the afternoon, and I wrote at night, although too often I was tempted away from my typewriter. Virgil and Louise LeQuire were very close friends. Jane and Louise had known each other in high school. Virgil had joined the department of anatomy the same year I was hired by the English department. Sometimes at night, when I should have been writing, we would ride around in one of our cars and drink whiskey from a bottle and enjoy being with each other. But mostly I worked from after dinner until bedtime, leaving Jane alone until I emerged from my study. A year or so after Pam was born, with Jane's mother's help, we bought a house for $11,000—living room, dining room, two bedrooms, two tiny baths, and a small den that I used as a study. These were lonely days for Jane, and she does not look back fondly at this period of our lives, but she endured that time without complaint.

Completing the manuscript was only a part of my problem. Like most other beginning writers, I needed a publisher, and I had only the vaguest idea of how to look for one. Before I graduated from Vanderbilt, I had met David Clay, who published Elizabeth Spencer's first novel, but I had no manuscript to show him at that time—probably fortunately so, since it would have been very bad—and several years passed before I thought I had something worth submitting. David McDowell, who had been at Kenyon with Peter Taylor and Cal Lowell and Randall Jarrell, was an editor at Random House. I had not met him, although I would later, but he knew Lon Cheney and Red Warren, so I sent him the yet to be completed manuscript of *Sojourn of a Stranger.* I know that some lucrative publishing contracts have been offered to first novelists by editors who have read only a chapter or two of a book. But I think that for me, and for most beginning writers, submitting a partial manuscript was and is a mistake. Even if you submit a précis of the full action of the book—which is dangerous because, if you follow a plan, you shut down the process of discovery that is essential to fiction—editors conceive their own ideas about how the rest of the novel should be written—ideas that never fully correspond with those of the writer. And, the theme and execution of the novel, which looked fresh when the editor first saw them, grow stale with time. While the writer writes, the editor works on other projects that engage his mind and turn his attention away from the partial manuscript that he read months earlier. In the end the completed manuscript is likely to be rejected.

At least, that's what happened to me. After months of my writing and their considering and an abundant correspondence between us, David informed me, "with great regret" and in "bitter disappointment," that Random House had rejected my novel. A letter from one of the in-house readers praising the novel at length and saying she had fought to have it published made me feel better, but not much. Nobody likes rejections. They hurt less as you continue to write and get acceptances as well as disappointments, but they are most painful at the beginning of your career, and, in my case, I needed to publish my novel not only to be a writer but also to continue my effort to be a professor. At Vanderbilt, Donald Davidson had made his way without a Ph.D., but I heard from one of my senior colleagues that Mr. Davidson was not sanguine about my ability to do the same—whether because he thought the academic situation had changed or because he thought I wasn't good enough, I never learned. But it seemed to me that with a wife and a baby and a mortgage, I had no choice but to continue teaching. I couldn't stop now and go back to graduate school. My and my family's future depended on my novel.

After the rejection by Random House, I submitted my manuscript to Harper's, and it was still there when Red Warren, kind and generous as always, came to my aid. He was in Nashville in May 1956 to attend a reunion of the Fugitive poets. He asked about my novel and offered to put me in touch with Helen Strauss, his agent at the William Morris Agency, in whom he had great confidence. "I can't make her take you as a client," Red said, "but if I ask her, she'll read your novel." He assured me that if she agreed to represent me, she would place my manuscript. This was good news indeed, but in a way, for Jane and me, it increased the tension. Now we waited to hear from Red or from Helen Strauss as well as from Harper's. Once more we watched anxiously for the postman, and after a couple of weeks I got a card from Red, who was in Italy. He had spoken to Helen. I could send her my book. We endured more waiting. Before I received any word from Helen, Harper's rejected the manuscript. But then I got from Helen a flattering letter accepting me as a client, and on the day before Thanksgiving she sent me a telegram. Holt had offered a contract with a $2,000 advance, more than a third of my year's salary as an assistant professor. Jane and I welcomed the money, but more than that we rejoiced in the security that publishing a book would bring.

The novel wasn't quite finished. Bob Lescher, my editor at Holt, asked for a new ending, and his request taught me my first lesson in the seemingly interminable business of writing a book. I was deeply weary. I had lived with my story and my characters for a long time. I had reworked and revised and rewritten, and I wanted to take a deep breath or two and move on to another project, but I had to admit that I wasn't quite finished with *Sojourn of a Stranger*. Fortunately, I got the manuscript and the editor's comments on it during Christmas vacation 1956. Bob Lescher had suggested revisions of various passages, but I decided that the best thing would be to discard the last 150 pages and write a new final sequence. For the rest of the Christmas vacation, I worked with more intensity than I ever had. I wrote in the mornings and in the afternoons. Now and then I left my smoke-filled study to step outside and breathe deeply, and when night came, my usual time for writing, I was exhausted. When I had to teach again, I kept working hard, and I had my new final pages ready to send back to Holt by the middle of February.

After the novel was finished and the manuscript accepted, with the proofs to come and August 1957 set as the date for publication, I tried to figure out what I had done right and what I had done wrong and what I had learned from the experience. I soon realized that I had used too many words, particularly in my descriptions of people and places. I wasn't sure about my dialogue. It seemed too formal, stilted sometimes, but my story was set in a previous time when people were more formal and spoke to each other with greater care and more respect. In the story some of the most effective parts were scenes that I had not anticipated, that had come to me in the process of writing. This kind of discovery has continued for me for the rest of my career, and I think it is common not only for novelists but also for poets. "No surprise for the writer," said Robert Frost, "no surprise for the reader." Every writer with whom I have ever talked would agree with this.

And what about my research? Had I really needed to read all those books about the Civil War, or had that been my way of avoiding the hard work of writing? I don't know. You never know what you're going to need until you need it. The only battle in my book is the battle of Franklin, and that occupies only a few pages. But fighting is not the only thing soldiers do. They march and make and break camp and take care of themselves and their equipment. They think and hope and anticipate the future. I believe that I needed to know what their lives were like, and I believe I learned as much as I was capable of learning from the books I read. Much later I returned to that period when I compiled *The War the Women Lived,* an anthology of excerpts from diaries of Confederate women. Reading and rereading those diaries, I found myself in a familiar ambience. I had been there before. I decided, right or wrong, that for my first novel I had needed to be there.

So I had a published book. I had tenure. I was reasonably safe at Vanderbilt for as long as I wanted to stay there. But, as I should have discovered when I was in Iowa and didn't, my beginning came at the end of an era that would leave me and most southern writers in confusion. We were no longer living in the South of the southern renascence.

Chapter Fourteen

Visitors from Far and Near

When I joined the Vanderbilt faculty in 1949, I was among friends who two years earlier had been my teachers. From almost as far back as I could remember, I had wanted to be a writer; after I entered Vanderbilt, I saw that, in order to write, I would have to teach, because, with a few exceptions, good writers didn't make much money from their writing. Now teaching was occupying much of my time, probably more than the forty hours a week that most people worked, but I was young and Jane was patient and we had faith in the future. We also enjoyed the people among whom we lived. Dr. Curry was still head of the English department. Mr. Davidson was still teaching and writing, as were Richmond Beatty and Claude Finney and Monroe Spears. Edgar Duncan still ran the freshman English program that taught those who didn't already know how to compose an English sentence, preparing them to go into their advanced courses and to write the papers they would be required to write. In my judgment, we were a good department, and we shared an admiration, almost a veneration, for literature recent and past, much of it written by white men, now dead, but some of it written by women who had lived in the past, most of them white too because

God had made them that color. We argued sometimes about whether Shakespeare was a greater writer than Chaucer or about whether a poem as hard to fathom as *The Waste Land* could be a great poem, but we never doubted the tradition in which we worked.

The college faculty was small enough for people from different departments to be friends. We had varying views of politics and culture and society, but with only a few exceptions we were civil with each other, and usually friendship would subordinate our differences. It would be wrong to say that we were one "happy family." We were several families, separate groups, but we were conscious of supporting each other in a common endeavor to educate our students and to convey to them the cultural and moral values that guided our work. The civil rights movement, with which most of the faculty sympathized, created at Vanderbilt less contention than confusion. At private universities outside the South, student populations were already racially integrated. The same was true for public institutions, but both private and public universities in the South remained segregated. After the Supreme Court decision in *Brown v. Board of Education,* black students sued successfully to be admitted to public universities, but, temporarily at least, private institutions, because they were not directly supported by the taxpayers, were immune from judicial authority. But the situation was by no means that simple. Vanderbilt alumni, most of whom were southerners, contributed to the endowment and to the operating expenses of the university. However, as a research university, Vanderbilt received grants from the federal government and from mostly northern, mostly liberal, foundations.

Although the trustees of the university were largely conservative, the majority of them were businessmen; for them, money talked. At lunch one day, one trustee, who was bitterly against integrating any part of the university, remarked, "They say that to get the gold, you have to take the black," punning on the Vanderbilt colors and shaking his head at the dilemma in which he found himself. Mr. Davidson was by far the most conservative of my colleagues. When he is remembered at all, he is recalled as a racist and a crackpot, but that simple description hardly fits his case. His views on segregation were not based solely on sentiment. He believed and thought he could demonstrate that there were differences between the races; even after the Supreme Court decision, he thought that, ultimately, he and his allies could litigate until some court, somewhere, would render judgments in their favor. This was very curious, because he was a brilliant man, more perceptive and more learned than almost anyone I ever knew. For a while, he worked with representatives of the White Citizens' Council, and one night, at his insistence, I joined him at the Hermitage Hotel to meet a leader of the council in Mississippi, a middle-aged man with a big stomach and a redolent cigar who was very angry at all federal authorities. I remained silent while he and Mr. Davidson discussed their mutual desire to defend the South and the southern tradition, but the man urged violence, something I had never heard Mr. Davidson advocate. This was not the kind of man with whom Mr. Davidson would ordinarily associate. This was not the sort of person with whom I had ever been friends. I sat and listened and wondered why I had come, what I had expected to see. I had no answer. I simply had come.

Nothing was said that night that I hadn't heard before, but I began to feel increasingly uncomfortable. I felt that something was wrong in the room, something unexplainable in mundane terms, something that made me want to leave, which I did as soon as I could, stepping out into the ordinary hotel corridor, riding down on an elevator with a man and a woman who smiled at each other and smiled at me as if all was right with the world. I crossed the lobby and went out the back door of the hotel onto a dimly lit and deserted Capitol Boulevard. Then a car carrying three white boys whom I had never seen before, and who, I am certain, had never before seen me, stopped beside me, and the boys began to curse me in terms that I hadn't heard since I left boot camp in the Marine Corps. The boys invited me to fight, threatening to beat me up whether I chose to fight or not. At first, I was more surprised than angry. I felt my jaw sag in astonishment. Then my anger started to build, but before I was sufficiently angry to make a casualty of myself, the boys, who were not very imaginative, ran out of words and drove away. I went to my car, shaken, but not so much so that I failed to see the irony of my situation. Were these three vulgar boys the avatars of Western civilization? Were they the guardians of the culture that all of us, liberal and conservative, hoped to save?

Early in his tenure as chancellor, which began in the 1950s, Harvie Branscomb persuaded Harold Vanderbilt, a grandson of Cornelius Vanderbilt, after whom the university was named, to join the Board of Trust. His wife, Gertrude, took an interest in the English department and promised to give $5,000 a year, a good sum in those pre-inflationary days, to hold an annual literary symposium. For the first couple of years, Randall Stewart organized the symposium; then I succeeded him, and my duties included consulting with Mrs. Vanderbilt, who said that if she liked what we were doing she would endow the sympo-sium, but she hadn't yet endowed it: every spring, I had to go to her, hat in hand. She was, in my judgment, a woman of peculiar tastes and sometimes even more curious opinions. Apparently, she thought a good deal about money. She told me once that the "real money" in her and Mr. Vanderbilt's family belonged to Mr. Vanderbilt. She had only ten million dollars of her own, this when money was worth much more than it is now. She worried about being cheated. When the grocery bill at her house in Palm Beach seemed too high, she dressed herself as a person of slender means and investigated prices at the grocery stores. Many people, she told me, many of whom did not deserve it, asked her for money. The inference of what she was saying was not lost on me.

The symposium was a rousing success. Not only the university com-munity but also people from all over Nashville came to hear visiting writers, to talk with them after their lectures or readings, and to have books signed. Without Mrs. Vanderbilt's support there would be no symposium, and I was determined to have it continue; I wanted des-perately to please Mrs. Vanderbilt, but my job would have been easier if I had known what she wanted me to say. If she had contended that the earth was flat, I would have agreed with alacrity and deplored the fact that everybody did not know this. Consequently, coward that I was, I did not dispute her when she said that it was all right to teach Shake-speare, but only selected passages. A whole play was too much to ask students to read. She told me that one of her prep school teachers in Philadelphia had asked her to memorize verses by Shelley, which she did, but she had declined to recite them because "wert" was not a word that anybody except Shelley used, and she would not join him in sub-verting the English language. I kept remembering Scott Fitzgerald's remark that the rich were different from the rest of us and Hemingway's riposte that they had more money, and I sided with Fitzgerald.

My major problem in dealing with Mrs. Vanderbilt was the difference between the cultures in which we had been bred. She gave money to the *Paris Review,* and she often praised George Plimpton, hoping, I suppose, that I would be more like him, but that was a lost cause. My southern manners, my southern accent, were the only ones I had, and it was too late for me to try to change them. But I did what I could. She once reprimanded me for using "school" to refer to a university. "Never do that," she cautioned. "School refers to your prep school. You call your college a college." I didn't make that mistake a second time. On one of her trips, she visited the English department offices, arriving with the thermos of martinis that she seemed always to carry in lieu of a purse. Randall was still our chairman, and I do not know why I didn't take Mrs. Vanderbilt to his office, but we went to Ed Duncan's more austere quarters, where we were joined by several of my colleagues. We got Mrs. Vanderbilt settled in the best chair available, took our places around her, and waited to try to answer whatever she might ask. To our discomfort, at first, she did not ask anything, but it was clear that she wanted something. She looked around, not at us, but at the door and the corners of the room. Finally, she put out her hand as if she expected whatever she needed to be put in it.

"Mrs. Vanderbilt," I said, "what may I get for you?"

"Water," she replied, her tone indicating that I was a fool for having to ask.

All of us scurried to find a glass in which to put the water—sooner said than done in this case, for most of us used the drinking fountains in the building. We got a glass from one of the secretaries, thick and clumsy and, I surmised, not the sort from which Mrs. Vanderbilt was accustomed to drink. But she did drink, and then she talked, and we agreed with whatever she said, whatever our thoughts were on the subject under discussion. Mercifully, the interview was soon over. I offered to accompany her to her car. "Well," she said, "you won't have far to go." And I didn't. Our building was in the middle of the campus, but her driver had brought her cross-country, over the lawns and walks and around trees, to park at our front door, which was where I said good-bye to her.

The symposium continued, and ultimately, perhaps in her will, Mrs. Vanderbilt endowed it, but this was after I had turned the program over to someone else. Randall Stewart had invited to the first symposia some of our distinguished alumni, members of the Fugitive and Agrarian groups who had brought notice, if not fame, to Vanderbilt in the late twenties and early thirties. Allen Tate, Robert Penn Warren, John Crowe Ransom, Andrew Lytle, and Cleanth Brooks appeared on some of the early programs, and, when I succeeded Randall, I invited them to come again. Alexander Heard, who had become chancellor when Harvie Branscomb retired, thought we were overdoing the Fugitive-Agrarian connection and said so. From time to time, Alex Heard got a letter from Jim Dickey asking that he be invited to read. Jim had earned an M.A. at Vanderbilt shortly after World War II. In his letters to Alex, he always warned that his schedule of readings was filling up. To avoid disappointment, we should invite him at once. He added that Vanderbilt ought to be "falling all over itself" to arrange for him to receive an honorary degree. Vanderbilt doesn't give honorary degrees, but frequently, after letters from Dickey, Alex suggested that I invite Jim to appear at a symposium, probably because he was tired of the letters Jim was writing him.

I held my ground. I knew Jim and how he behaved too well for me to take responsibility for him, but the story has a sequel. Dan Young, my successor at running the symposium, in innocence or with guile, for Dan was known as a campus politician and may have wanted to curry favor with Alex Heard, invited Dickey and appointed a graduate student to be Jim's keeper. The student's duties were, first, to get Jim to the auditorium in time for the reading, and, second, to keep Jim sufficiently sober to read his own lines, an assignment that only a policeman and a tough one at that could have accomplished. At the hour that the program was to begin, students crowded the auditorium. Some were there because they admired Jim's poetry. Many more had read his novel *Deliverance* or seen the movie based on it. They occupied all the seats, stood at the back and along the walls, sat or sprawled in the aisles, but there was no Dickey. Dan Young hastened to the Holiday Inn where Jim was staying, went immediately to the bar, and found Jim and the graduate student drinking together. I did not see the scene that followed. Later, Dan said that the graduate student was drunk beyond taking care of himself, much less seeing that Dickey kept to his schedule. Jim was at first happy, but he soon resented the tone in which Dan spoke to him.

He declared that he was not ready to leave the bar and might not leave at all unless Dan addressed him in more conciliatory terms. He agreed to come at once when Dan threatened to withhold his stipend.

In a perfect world, Jim would have paid for his arrogance with a poor reading and a disgusted audience, but no such thing happened. After his introduction, he mounted the stage with a firm step. He stood behind the dais silently allowing his gaze to move from one side of the room to the other, letting the audience wait a moment longer in anticipation. Then in the loudest voice he could muster, he said, "Sh-i-i-t," drawing out the word that, to the best of my recollection, had never before been spoken from a Vanderbilt stage by a visiting writer. He paused for a moment, beaming at the audience. He was having his triumph, congratulating himself for having packed the hall. The delighted students cheered this contravention of protocol. When they quieted down, Jim read and read well.

I brought to Vanderbilt the best writers I could find who would agree to come. Among fiction writers who lectured and read were Anthony Burgess, William Golding, Allen Sillitoe, Elizabeth Spencer, Eudora Welty, Jean Stafford, Peter Taylor, Mary Lavin, Katherine Anne Porter, J. F. Powers, Flannery O'Connor, Shelby Foote, Walker Percy, Madison Jones, Verlin Cassill, Andrew Lytle, and Benedict Kiely, who lingered in Nashville several days beyond the agreed time, lecturing to classes and seeing the sights and being convivial. One morning, Ben was scheduled to speak to a large class I taught, and about 10:30 I went to the old Anchor Motel to take him to the classroom. All seemed well until Ben suggested that, before we left, we should have a drink, a notion that brought me to a professional, if not a moral, crisis. I had never had a drink before meeting a class, I didn't think I should have one now, but Ben was to give the lecture, not I, so I agreed to have one. Ben got his bottle of Jameson—how many of those he drank while he was in Nashville, I couldn't guess, all purchased by the English department with Mrs. Vanderbilt's money. We had only the glasses that motels furnished at that time, thick and ugly, but sufficiently commodious. I took no more than would fill a jigger; Ben took enough to fill his glass. Well, I thought, here is disaster. But, before my thought was completed, Ben drank and poured generously and drank again and declared himself ready. I believed I was in for trouble, but that was not the case. Ben mounted the stage without a stagger, allowed me to hang the lavalier microphone around his neck, and lectured in clear and well-enunciated Irish tones that charmed the students. The class was scheduled to end at noon. The tower clock struck verifying the hour, but nobody left. The students waited until Ben was through. Then they stood and applauded.

Some poets who read at Vanderbilt were Richard Wilbur, Richard Eberhart, W. H. Auden, Louis Coxe, Louis Simpson, Donald Justice, Paul Engle, William Stafford, William Jay Smith, Robert Hollander, and those stalwarts from the Fugitive days, John Crowe Ransom, Allen Tate, and Robert Penn Warren. In spite of legendary topers such as Dylan Thomas and madmen like Cal Lowell, in my limited experience as a literary impresario I found that, in general, poets, while not abstemious, behaved more prudently than novelists. Allen Tate was an exception. He drank too much and chased too many women and married too many times, but his fellow Fugitives, Mr. Ransom and Red Warren, lived careful lives, husbanding their energy as if, wherever they were and whatever they were doing, a part of their minds was always at work on the poem or novel or essay that they were writing. For most of the years that I knew him, Mr. Davidson did not drink at all. His life after the Fugitive movement had been different from those of his colleagues, more difficult, as he saw it, and he seemed to want to separate himself from the loose behavior of other writers, from any suggestion of bohemian excess.

Some writers visited us for entire semesters, but these did not come on Mrs. Vanderbilt's money; they were supported by outside foundations such as the American Council of Learned Societies or they substituted for Vanderbilt professors who were on leave and were paid out of the department budget. Our Fugitive standbys, Ransom, Tate, and Lytle, each came for a term. One of my brightest memories is of Mr. Ransom and Mr. and Mrs. Davidson having dinner with Jane and me on a bitterly cold night that followed a hard rain and made our driveway treacherous. Mr. Davidson complained about the ice, but he soon followed Mr. Ransom's example, had a drink, and, with Mr. Ransom, began to reminisce about old days in Nashville when every street was safe and most places were within walking distance of one another and a "pie wagon"—

we still used the term to refer to small restaurants—was pulled by mules every night to a location on Broad Street and pulled back before dawn to wherever it spent the day. Although there was no love lost between Edwin Mims and the Fugitives, Mr. Ransom and Mr. Davidson sometimes joined a group that walked to town to have lunch with him on Saturday.

V. S. Pritchett and his wife, Dorothy, spent two separated semesters at Vanderbilt. They occupied a small house at the edge of the campus and depended on friends to drive them to most places they wanted to go. Dorothy favored a taxi driver who took her on utilitarian errands, to the grocery store or the shoe shop or the druggist. She always referred to him as "Yellow Cab driver number 17," and he was the only one she would patronize. On one of Victor's visits to Vanderbilt, he introduced Eudora Welty at a session of the literary symposium, praising her highly, as she deserved.

"There," Eudora said. "Now you've heard it from the horse's mouth," which indeed we had. That night, two of the most gifted story writers alive sat on the same stage. Unlike some others who came to Vanderbilt, Victor wore his literary fame lightly. He had begun his life in the family leather business, and he was almost as proud of his ability to judge animal hides as he was of his literary prowess.

Over the years, our long-term visitors came from various parts of the world, and most of them spoke English fluently. In one spectacular case, we were joined for a semester by a Japanese novelist who, we were told, was "the Robert Penn Warren of Japan." He appeared to be capable of speaking only two English sentences. "Do you know Allen Tate?" he would ask, and when you said that you did, he would smile amiably and say, "Thank you very much."

His wife knew English quite well, but she would not admit that she knew it when he was close by. She would not translate for him. She would not take messages over the phone. At parties, when he was at one end of a room and she was at the other, she would chat easily, but when he approached, suddenly, with a straight face she would say that she did not speak English. This was trying, but, once, her refusal to translate for her husband brought what some of us considered just retribution. They were at our house. To go with her food, Jane had put out some mild mustard and some that was extremely hot. Our visitor chose the hot and began to pile it on his ham and biscuit.

"Please," Jane said to his wife, "he is welcome to all he wants of anything, but that mustard is very hot. Please tell him. He will burn himself."

His wife, giving Jane an innocent smile, said, "No speak."

The Robert Penn Warren of Japan took a large bite. His eyes filled with tears. His face turned a deep red. He began to gasp. Jane gave him water, which did not immediately cool the fire. Our guest gasped again and coughed and wheezed. No one could help him. We watched while he suffered. But nothing changed. His pain wasn't sufficiently severe for him to allow his wife to translate for him.

Chapter Fifteen

New Directions

Randall Stewart had come from Brown to be our chairman after Dr. Curry retired, and with his coming we entered a period so peaceful that most of our complaints to each other were about indolent students and the college administration, about wicked politicians and treacherous weather, but almost never about decisions Randall had made. He was in charge of the courses we taught and when we taught them, of the promotions we got and when we got them, of our salaries and our leaves and our trips to professional meetings. When Jack Aden wondered why Randall had hired an assistant professor without consulting the senior members of the department, Randall smiled and said, "It's an imperfect world," which disarmed Jack and gave him another story to tell as only he could tell it. Randall was a great raconteur too, and he could talk at length on almost any subject.

Once, when Randall and I were returning from Atlanta, we stopped on the way to our gate in the airport to have a martini. Randall liked martinis, particularly those that were as well concocted as the one we had turned out to be. From before we left the bar until we arrived on the plane Randall praised the martini as a major blessing of modern civilization. He spoke of good ones he had had and of a few that were mediocre. He pondered the virtues of vermouth and told sadly of some-one he had known who had mixed gin with Dubonnet, in Randall's judgment perhaps not a sin but, at best, a culpable miscalculation. Randall had a ruddy complexion that sometimes made him seem flushed to those who did not know him—which on this occasion included the head stewardess. She heard Randall speak in joyful anticipation of the martini we meant to have on the way home, and she declined to sell liquor, not only to us, but to all the passengers. "It's an imperfect world," Randall said of our dry flight home. He switched his conversation on martinis to another subject.

In the late fifties Randall's health began to fail, and the charitable nature of Vanderbilt as an institution worked against us. Randall had a series of small strokes that dimmed his mind and left him unable to make decisions, but the college administrators kept Randall in place and offered neither him nor the rest of us any assistance. The old hu-morous light had gone out of Randall's eyes. Day after day, he sat at his desk with pen and paper in front of him. Occasionally he wrote a few sentences that developed no thought and seemed to have little rela-tionship to one another. He had agreed to give a paper at the meeting in the fall of 1961 of the South Atlantic Modern Language Association, known as SAMLA, and to participate in a panel to discuss writing biog-raphy. Randall had been a distinguished scholar when he was younger. His biography of Hawthorne had been widely praised, and, after he ar-rived at Vanderbilt, he wrote a book on American literature and Chris-tianity that undertook less than the title promised but was logical and well written and fairly well reviewed. Now, with his brain damaged, he could write only four or five pages for his SAMLA presentation, which was scheduled to last twenty minutes. The ideas he was able to reclaim from his memory were simple, and the language he used to express them was simple as well. His paper was not good, but it was the best he could do, and when he asked me to make the trip to Atlanta and deliver it for him, I was glad to agree. In innocence I went.

I had been in the profession for more than a decade. I had seen aca-demic politics at work. I was aware of the deep envy that existed be-tween some scholars and critics. No doubt, in better days, some were jealous of Randall. Now his debility was known throughout the profession. He was no longer able to attack others or to defend himself. It seemed to me then and seems to me now that he deserved to be treated with the dignity that his past work had earned, or simply with the charity that one human being owes another.

His colleagues on the panel—my colleagues now—were bibliographers: one, Fredson Bowers, was old and famous and notorious; the other, James Meriwether, was young and ambitious and, as I had seen before and would see later, not afflicted by charity, which might have impeded his rise in the world. But this puts me ahead of my story. I was called on to read first. I mentioned Randall's illness in general terms to explain my presence at the meeting. I read Randall's paper in less time than had been scheduled for it. Then I listened while his and my fellow panelists attacked what Randall had said. Or more than this. They condemned not only his poor present effort, but most of his work as well, essays and books that he had written when he was younger and his mind was whole. I was helpless to defend him. I didn't know enough about American literature and Hawthorne and the art of writing biography to make a case on his behalf.

With Randall still in place as chairman but unable to do his job, the department drifted. The ordinary housekeeping decisions that needed to be made every year—what courses, particularly sections of freshman English, would be offered and when they would meet and who would teach them—were not made. Letters that concerned the department went unanswered. Nobody represented us when department heads met with college administrators and budgets were devised. Cyrus Hoy, who was on leave, received a job offer from the University of Rochester. Cyrus did not want to leave Vanderbilt, and, I think, he did not expect to. He waited to receive a counteroffer from Vanderbilt, but the counteroffer would have to be written by the chairman and forwarded through two or three layers of bureaucracy, and Randall was too ill to do what he needed to do. Cyrus, still away from our campus and under pressure from the authorities at Rochester, waited as long as he thought he could. So we lost Cyrus. A few months later, Randall retired. Ed Duncan served as our interim chairman until a new chairman was appointed.

Was it because we liked Randall so much that we liked Russell Fraser so little? Did some of us realize, if only subconsciously, that when Randall died our golden years went with him? Whatever our more complicated motives might have been, we all resented that we had no part in hiring Russell; the dean had hired him for us. Russell was one of several candidates who had visited our campus, but we never met to vote on whom we would like our next chairman to be. We never saw the correspondence between Russell and the dean, but the explanation that the dean gave the department made clear what had happened. Russell pressed the dean for a decision. He claimed that he had other offers to consider, including a fine one from Princeton, where he was then employed. He was well disposed toward Vanderbilt and would likely accept the job as our chairman if the terms offered were satisfactory. But he could not wait. He had to have a decision and have it now. So, without consulting members of the department, the dean offered Russell the chairmanship, and he took it.

Allen Tate, who was interested in whatever went on in the literary world, and who was particularly interested in Vanderbilt, where he had studied and lectured and served as a visiting professor, disapproved of the Fraser appointment even before he met Russell. "Remember, Walter," he said, "Princeton never lost anybody they really wanted to keep." Whether that was true or not, Princeton was too much on Russell's mind when he got to Vanderbilt. He knew that we could never be Princeton, that we could never truly mimic it in the depth and breadth of our course offerings or in the overall distinction of our faculty. He thought that we might duplicate Princeton's program in the literature of the English renaissance, which was Russell's field, and, insofar as possible, given that many books on the subject were out of print, buy for our library copies of the same materials on the renaissance that were in the Firestone Library at Princeton. Russell's proposal did not threaten me. The books I wanted for our library were contemporary novels and volumes of criticism. The courses in writing that we offered were substantially the same as those offered at other institutions. But members of the department who did research and taught courses in other periods were affronted. With a limited budget with which to add to our library holdings, professors who worked in medieval and romantic and Victorian literature wanted books in their own specialties.

Following the example set by the dean, Russell hired Leonard Nathanson without seeking our approval. One of the reasons he gave for hiring Leonard was that he thought we "needed a Jew" on our faculty—a bad reason for hiring in any event but, more important, an insult both to us and to Leonard. Leonard was such a generous and interesting colleague that we were delighted to have him, but for us the happy end of this appointment didn't justify the means. We continued to be wary, if not hostile, toward Russell. To give him the credit he deserves, he tried, as best he knew how, to bring peace to the department. He asked us to dinner, and we entertained him and his wife. He sought our opinions and our votes on departmental decisions by mail, but this fueled our suspicions. Why did he not want us to meet as a group to exchange opinions and ask questions? What was this polling by mail an attempt to hide? One night we met at his house, where he served us good brandy bought at a duty-free shop, but he was visibly distressed—and, I think, justifiably—by how much we drank. The evening did nothing to ameliorate our distrust of each other.

Near the end of his tenure at Vanderbilt, when he probably had already started looking for another job, Russell brought Kingsley Amis, whom he knew well, to our campus. Again, he did not consult his faculty. Kingsley's wife, Jane, came too, and they were immediately popular in Nashville. People liked Kingsley's accent, the cut of his English clothes, the gold and porcelain antique boxes in which he carried his snuff. He was amiable and interesting, good company, as was Jane, and they were entertained by the faculty and by Lon and Fannie Cheney, who were the uncrowned heads of Nashville literary society, and by Jean and Alex Heard, the Vanderbilt chancellor, who introduced them to people who were not well schooled in literature but some of whom were interesting and all of whom were rich, and they entertained well. Jane was herself a novelist, Elizabeth Jane Howard, but none of her novels was as famous as Kingsley's *Lucky Jim,* and most of those whom she met outside the academic world did not know that she was a writer. Partially because of this, Jane found few companions among the women of Nashville, and, although she was writing, she said little about what she was writing or how it progressed. What appeared to be old frictions in her relationship with Kingsley occasionally arose.

Late one afternoon when the Amises were riding home with my Jane and me, we began to talk of World War I. Somebody mentioned Sir Douglas Haig, who had commanded British forces in 1914. "Oh, yes," Jane said, "I remember him. He used to come to tea when I was a little girl."

Kingsley was immediately angry. "God damn it!" he said, "there you go again! You do me this way all the time!"

Jane did not reply. In the brief silence that followed, it came to me, belatedly to say the least, who Jane was: a Howard, a member of one of the oldest and most distinguished families in England, where social differences count for more than they do in the United States.

The moment soon passed. Jane Sullivan, ever diplomatic and quick-witted, started us on a new subject. Kingsley suppressed his anger. We were lighthearted again

Kingsley's appointment at Vanderbilt was for one semester, a little more than three months, and Jane and I were sorry to see him and Jane leave. We had enjoyed their company. We considered them friends, and we hoped to see them on our next trip to England. But soon after she and Kingsley got home, Jane published an article in the *Sunday Telegraph* that condemned Nashville and Tennessee and the South. Her occasion for writing was the assassination of Martin Luther King, which had occurred in Memphis and about which she knew only what she had read in the newspapers. But Dr. King's death was no surprise to her, she wrote, because of the climate of racism that she had encountered in Nashville. Her article consisted mostly of dialogue, a compendium of clichés that denigrated blacks. She said she had heard daily, sometimes hourly, of the incompetence and laziness of black people, of their inability to survive without white guidance, of their childlike qualities that endowed them with engaging personalities but that made it necessary for white people to devise and enforce rules for their behavior.

In a way what Jane wrote of Nashville was true. The remarks that she quoted had been made, and the attitudes that she attributed to those who made them were described accurately. Jane had met people from old Nashville families. Portraits of their forebears, many in Confederate uniforms, hung in their living rooms. They had heard from their grandmothers how the silver with which their dinner guests now ate had been hidden from marauding federal troops by loyal slaves. This was a fragment of the truth about the South, as Jane's rendition of southern racism was a part of the truth about the South. Like the representatives of the old Confederate families—not neo-Confederates, since they had never abandoned the cause—Jane Howard pursued her own ends. She urged racial justice by the stories that she told. But it seemed to me that

Jane, novelist as she was, would know that no world is as simple and as simply divided between the good and the bad as the world of the South that she depicted.

She was, I think, acting out the role of a woman scorned. In Nashville, Kingsley had been a star. Those of his new acquaintances who had not read his work bought his books and displayed them on their coffee tables. They told each other that Kingsley was famous. They introduced him to their friends as a talented and successful writer. They all had heard that Jane wrote too, and that was how they thought of it: that she followed meekly along in Kingsley's footsteps. Even among the Vanderbilt faculty as a whole, some of whom, at least, knew better, Jane's accomplishments as a novelist were largely ignored. The English department never asked her to give a reading. She appeared before a few small groups, book clubs that were composed, she thought, of dense people who asked stupid questions. She made clear in her article for the *Telegraph* that she thought the Vanderbilt faculty was largely composed of racist fools.

Chapter Sixteen

The Old Order Changeth

During the last few months of Russell Fraser's tenure as chairman of the Vanderbilt English department, we, his colleagues, waited, hoping and praying that he would leave. A psychology professor, once at Vanderbilt, then at Michigan, telephoned Jack Aden, who assured him that Russell had a nice disposition and an even temper. Later Jack said, "I hated to do that to old Stan, but somebody did it to us."

It seemed that Russell would receive an offer from Michigan, but would he take it? From somewhere we got a copy of a letter that a member of the Michigan English department had sent to Russell. We read it without shame. This was war, and all was fair, but the letter, encouraging Russell to come to Michigan, did not encourage us. It said that the offer from Michigan to Russell did not promise a significantly higher salary or better benefits than Russell received at Vanderbilt. The correspondent, whom many of us had met, promised Russell a friendly environment and colleagues who would appreciate his work. We at Vanderbilt waited. If Russell was going to leave, he would have to accept Michigan's offer by the end of the term. Every day the end of the term drew closer. We were well into spring, the weather warm, our world beginning to blossom. Time flew and time stood still. The end of the semester was getting uncomfortably nearer; waiting for Russell to make up his mind was getting on our nerves. Finally we heard that Russell had written a letter to be sent individually to members of the department. Again with no feeling of shame, I consulted the secretary who handled Russell's correspondence, but he had directed her to tell no one the contents of the letter until all copies were delivered.

Unfairly I pressed her. "Will I be happy when I read it?"

"Yes," she said, "I think you will."

And so I was. Russell left, and his erstwhile colleagues celebrated. But divisions that had perhaps been hidden during Russell's tenure now were manifest. Our department split into two parties: the old and the young. We disagreed on appointments and promotions and course offerings. Our new chairman was not Jack Aden but Dan Young, and Jack, although he bore his disappointment with grace, was deeply offended. Some of us wanted to invite Cleanth Brooks, who had recently retired from Yale, to teach a term at Vanderbilt, but the young professors, now a majority of the department, said no. Cleanth never forgave us. He returned several times to lecture, but he gave neither manuscripts nor books to the Heard Library, and he did not consider Vanderbilt or Nashville for a headquarters when he and Louis Rubin founded the Fellowship of Southern Writers.

In spite of the attempts by generations of faculty and students to move it into the modern world, Vanderbilt as a corporate entity dragged its feet. Russell Fraser, with his enduring loyalty to Princeton, was hardly the first to urge us to change. During meetings of the department, of the faculty, and of the faculty council we were kept abreast of what occurred in the Ivy League. Harvard taught freshman English this way; there was a new program at Yale. We were told how students at Michigan were taught, how the writing programs at Iowa and Stanford proceeded, what pedagogical innovations shaped studies at Texas, at Berkeley, but not in the English department at Vanderbilt. One reason for this was the layers of bureaucracy that delayed our actions and frustrated our desires. Once we wanted to hire a professor at Maryland: he had sent us his credentials, he had lectured on our campus, he had met our deans and other administrators, and we had asked, by formal correspondence, as was required, that our dean offer him a job. Whether he would have come to Vanderbilt under any circumstances is doubtful. Harvard wanted him and could outbid us in prestige as well as in money, but the way Harvard conducted its business should have been a lesson to us. While our proposal made its tardy way through deans and committees, the president of Harvard called the candidate, took him to lunch in Washington, and said, somewhat redundantly, "I'm the president of Harvard. Tell me what you want, and I will tell you whether I can give it to you. I can tell you right now."

The institutional procrastination of the Vanderbilt administration delayed our entry into the modern academic world, but it did not save us. Early in my career, I read an essay by Malcolm Cowley, but not really so much an essay as an ironic translation into plain English of an article written in jargon and published in a journal devoted to sociology. Once translated, the article said that rich people live in big houses; poor people live in small houses. By examining aerial photographs of a city, you can locate neighborhoods where the rich and the poor people live. This was in the early or middle 1950s. I knew that sociologists were not the only culprits. Art criticism had developed its own corrupt vocabulary. Practitioners in other disciplines, often the social sciences, were inventing new terminologies. How lucky we are, I thought. We who teach English know about language. We know about words. We know that jargon tends toward abstraction, abstraction is the enemy of clarity, and clarity is the queen of literary virtues. We who teach others how to write know how to practice what we preach. But I was wrong again. Soon came structuralism and deconstructionism and all the other isms to which many of my colleagues succumbed. As a department, we ceased to be "warders of the gate," as Mr. Davidson had called us; we joined the barbarians in their assault on logic and language.

For a while my own situation was not changed. I had given up my large lecture classes in modern British and American fiction in the late 1960s, partly because I wanted more direct contact with my students, partly because I could see in the disorder created by dissident students and faculty at other universities what Vanderbilt's future was likely to be. Quit when you're ahead, I told myself: I did, and, during the last years of my career, I taught only fiction writing, two sections of fifteen students each, both fall and spring. But, as Conrad's Axel Heyst learned to his sorrow, there is no escape from the world that surrounds you. We had weekly departmental meetings that I was required to attend, meetings where, it seemed to me, we spent most of our time plotting the overthrow of the culture that had nourished us. My colleagues—not only the young, but many who were old enough to know better—demanded that works written by "dead white men" be replaced in our curriculum by novels and poems written by women and by people of color, colored women preferred, but men acceptable. Sexual relations of all kinds became important literary themes. In my naïveté, I supposed there were restraints, limits, borders of decency that responsible writers and critics would not cross, but again I was mistaken.

One day I tried to convince a writing class that the possibilities for innovation when writing about sexual practice were limited. There were a lot more ways to commit murder, I told my class, than there were ways to make love, so it was easier to write innovatively about homicide than about fornication. I pointed out that, once ordinary sex became commonplace in novels, it became repetitious. Writers had to move on—to homosexuality, to sadomasochism, as each method of satisfying carnal desire became stale from the reader's familiarity with it. "You can trace our literary history," I said, "by looking at the covers of paperback novels. First there is the scantily clad woman, then two scantily clad women or two scantily clad men, then a woman in boots and a leather brassiere brandishing a whip most threateningly." All we had left, I told my students, was necrophilia, and surely nobody wants to read or write about that. Evidence to the contrary came in the next day's campus mail.

One of my friends of more enlightened taste than I sent me his old copies of the *Evergreen Review,* which printed boldly uncensored stories and essays that presented sex and sex acts as a kind of theology for the modern world. It printed a cartoon strip named for the heroine thereof, Phoebe Zeitgeist. In the previous episode Phoebe had been killed, shot full of arrows by a band of Buddhist monks. Now, her readers discovered, she really was dead, not rescued at the last minute, as had been the case in earlier chapters that chronicled her adventures. Her corpse had been snatched by a band of capitalists from Terre Haute, Indiana, and carried by limousine to a secret subterranean vault where she became part of a collection of nude female bodies that were preserved and mechanized and used to satisfy the unwholesome desires of the bankers who had filched them. What was I to say to my students, not only about being proved wrong so decisively, but also about why I, self-appointed keeper of the moral truth, had been reading about the scandalous Phoebe? There was no satisfactory explanation for that and still isn't. I availed myself of the usual human excuse. I was not the subscriber to the magazine, which, I implied, mitigated my responsibility. This was not true, of course, but I consoled myself with the knowledge that I had to confess to my class that I had been wrong. My mistake about the limits of human depravity, in which I had participated, was my punishment.

At Vanderbilt, the department of English was organized after other departments—classics, mathematics, theology—had been established. When a major in English was offered, it followed the dominant ages of English literature, as the requirements for majoring in English did then at most universities. There were courses in the literature of the Anglo-Saxon period, the renaissance, the restoration, the eighteenth and nineteenth centuries. In the senior year, a comprehensive course reviewed the literature of all periods and attempted to show the relationship of one literary age to another. As time passed, additions to the program were made—courses in fiction writing, poetry writing, literary criticism—but until the upheavals of the 1960s and 1970s, the historical structure of the major remained intact. Significant changes came when we hired faculty members who were deconstructionists, who believed that not even the writer knew what his poem or novel meant; that meaning in language was impossible to establish. Nothing was final; nothing was absolute. The emphasis on works of literature viewed as comprehensible works of art shifted, as I have said, to a search for paraliterary themes: sexual attitudes and practices in all dimensions; racism; writings by members of cultures other than English or American. Long-forgotten texts were rediscovered, principally books by women, by homosexuals of either gender, by blacks or Amerindians or anyone who had lived in what was judged to be an oppressive society. People newly out of graduate school and newly hired by Vanderbilt were allowed to organize new courses that would explore popular sexual or cultural or social themes: "The Oppression of Women in the Novels of D. H. Lawrence," for example, or the institution of slavery as it was chronicled in such novels as *Uncle Tom's Cabin*. Courses in the plays of Shakespeare, when they were offered at all, sought to turn ordinary characters into sexual deviants and discovered in the lines they spoke hidden meanings that had escaped even Bowdler's accusing eye. With a limited number of faculty members, the department could offer only a limited number of courses. With no one willing to teach them, the traditional courses that were established according to literary periods began to die. We hired new faculty members to suit our altered circumstances—not to teach the literary periods that would complete our traditional set of offerings, but to plan and offer courses designed according to the interests or the prejudices of the teacher.

Traditional values, which survived under duress if at all in English departments, were under assault in churches as well. Jane and I had been raised as Methodists, but after we returned to Vanderbilt we joined the Episcopal Church, drawn there by the mysteries of Christianity and by the beauty of the liturgy. The first Book of Common Prayer, which was the basis not only of liturgical worship but also of the theology of the Anglican Church, was published in 1542. This edition was superseded in 1549 and again in 1559, which was during the golden age of English literature: the age of Shakespeare and Christopher Marlowe and Ben Jonson and their distinguished contemporaries; the age that produced the King James translation of the Bible. If the worship of God is the highest calling of human beings, as Christians believe, then worship, both private and public, should be conducted in words that are sufficiently beautiful and magisterial to fit their lofty purpose. From time to time during the centuries that followed its original publication, the Book of Common Prayer was revised, but the beauty of its language was left intact, as was the basic theology that undergirded the liturgy until the 1960s, when a radical rewriting of the prayer book began.

This was undertaken by theologians, many of them members of faculties at seminaries, to cleanse the liturgy of archaic language, thereby making it more intelligible to ordinary parishioners. But changing the liturgy meant changing the dogma of the church. The old words of the liturgy meant what they said. To make them clearer was also to reduce their meanings and to vitiate the faith that they proclaimed. The revisers of the 1960s and 1970s said in their writings, their homilies, their com-

ments in meetings of commissions and committees, that no article of
the Christian faith was sacrosanct: not the Virgin birth, not the Resur-
rection, not the miracles performed by Christ. My beloved and distinguished colleagues in the Vanderbilt English department, Jack Aden
and Hal Weatherby, were also Episcopalians, and they were concerned,
as I was, about the very survival of the Anglican faith. We were southerners, Jack and I born in the first quarter of the twentieth century.
Hal was a little younger, but all of us had roots in the mystical, mythical
South, the South that when we were growing up was acutely conscious
of its separateness from the rest of the nation. By inheritance, we were
the guardians of lost causes. According to the principles of the Christian
faith that we confessed and attempted to practice, we felt obliged to try
to save the Book of Common Prayer. Deep in our hearts, we all knew
that we could not do so, but, we told ourselves, somebody had to try.
We could not allow the church we loved to pass into history while we
watched and did not attempt to preserve it in all its piety and beauty.

Jack and Hal and I began our defense of the prayer book by recruiting
a few people in Nashville, then a few more at Sewanee, then a great
many more through advertisements in church publications. We gave
ourselves an infelicitous name, The Society for the Preservation of the
Book of Common Prayer, which we soon shortened to SPBCP. We established a mailing list that grew rapidly. We began a newsletter for our
members, and our members sent us money on which to operate. We
never had to beg, and the funds we collected were sufficient for us to
rent an office, hire a small staff, and travel to meetings with other traditional Episcopalians. But we struggled against a clever bureaucracy. The
presiding bishop of the church, elected to that office by his fellow bishops, is chairman of all the bishops and by extension of the body of the
church. His powers are limited by the actions of the House of Bishops
and the House of Deputies, both of which meet once every three years
to pass rules concerning church governance and to tinker with theology
in any way they please. The House of Bishops is composed of all who
hold episcopal rank; the deputies, some clerical, some lay, are elected by
the dioceses. Most of the deputies, even those in orders, are politicians,
not theologians. The priests are often rectors of large parishes. The laymen are lawyers, insurance men, bankers, people who deal with the

public, become well known in their communities, and usually contribute generously to the church. They get along well with bishops and priests, and in almost all matters they follow the lead of the clergy.

In 1970, the general convention of the Episcopal Church, which Jack, Hal, and I attended, met in Louisville. At the opening ceremony, bishops and priests from Catholic and Orthodox communions donned their colorful vestments and walked side by side down the aisle with the presiding bishop of the Episcopalians. For an hour, it was as if no divisions marred the unity of Christendom. Choirs sang. Bishops and priests and prominent laymen welcomed us and offered intercessions that had been carefully composed, stripped of phrases that might offend anyone present. The bishops delivered their innocuous invocations and prayers of dismissal. Then the bishops led us out of the church, and the next day the convention got down to business.

First there was a communion service held in a large gymnasium. There were seats on the ground level, and more seats in the first and second balconies that looked down at the temporary altar that had been erected on the floor. Throughout the gymnasium, at locations apparently judged to be most accessible to the worshipers, large pitchers of wine and patens stacked with communion wafers rested on small tables. Distributing the wine would be an inconvenience later—much later, because it took a long time for the processions from the various dioceses to enter and take their seats. Together they were a large and motley crowd. Some of the clergy were "high church" and wore vestments; some were "low church" and wore cassocks. Acolytes from the highest churches carried crucifixes. All groups were led by crosses of one kind or another, and there were several kinds of crosses: Roman crosses, patriarchal crosses, crosses of Lorraine. Many were decorated with flags and pennants, with stuffed animals dangling from the cross arms and with glass ornaments of different colors: clear glass angels with wings spread; animals that I took to be deer and rabbits and donkeys, some of them made of clear glass, some of red and green and blue. Small bells were hung from the crosses too, their rings too weak to penetrate the tones of the portable organ and the murmur of general conversation that persisted, even though the service had begun. Some of the marchers carried signs that urged delegates to the convention to modernize the prayer book, to vote to ordain women, to support labor unions in California, to save forests and the birds and animals that lived therein.

The individual processions milled about, entwined themselves with each other, and tried to reform their lines. Any system for orderly entry that had been devised by those who planned the service had failed in its execution. Inevitably, people bumped the tables. Wine, as yet unconsecrated, splashed on the tables and the floor and over the unconsecrated bread. Groups who had lost their way were obliged to wait for others to pass before they could retrace their footsteps. Chaos gradually subsided. At last everyone was seated. The volume of general conversation fell. A bishop welcomed us to the general convention and to the celebration of the Eucharist. After the bishop had finished the opening prayer, men and women of various races read the lessons, some in English, some in Spanish, some in languages or dialects that I could not place. The ceremony proceeded. The time for the distribution of communion came. Distributors brought chalices to the small tables to be filled with wine from the pitchers, and once more the wine, which was now consecrated, was spilled. It ran across the tables and made puddles and streaks on the gymnasium floor. Some hosts fell too, but most of these were recovered by distributors and acolytes, and the service continued.

We had rented a booth for the convention that was situated with other booths where purveyors of vestments and altar vessels and comparable items displayed their wares, and booths where organizations distributed literature and asked for money. Our booth was kept by volunteers from Louisville; by members of our staff who had come from Nashville; by Hal and Jack and Jane, when she could be away from her teaching job at Aquinas College in Nashville; and by me. We offered to those who visited our booth lapel buttons bearing the initials of the society or the smiley faces that we put on much of our literature or the words that became our mantra: "Save the prayer book, save the faith." We were not totally an amateur organization. The head of the art department at a Louisville advertising agency had joined us, and we profited from his help and his advice. We distributed well-written and well-designed brochures that described our cause and asked for support. We became acquainted with some of those who manned neighboring booths, some of whom were sympathetic to our cause, but, in most cases, they were paid staff whose loyalty was required by the people who paid them. We made some converts, but not a sufficient number to advance our cause.

Much of the work of the convention was done by committees that met in the mornings before the two houses that met separately were called to order. Jack and Hal and I attended meetings of the committee that was in charge of revising the prayer book. We listened, but without an official role in the convention we could not speak while the committee was in session. This made no difference. Our cause was so dismally lost from the outset that nothing we could have said would have changed the minds of many delegates. One sensible man from Nashville, a graduate of Vanderbilt, talked to Jack and Hal and me amiably and with apparent goodwill, but he thought that being loyal to the leaders of the church was more important than any damage that would result to the church if the Book of Common Prayer was titivated. Members of the SPBCP believed, rightly as it turned out, that if the new liturgy was adopted many Episcopalians would leave the church. Two or three years after the Louisville convention, Jack and Hal and I had an audience with the presiding bishop. When he had made clear what we already knew—that he was firmly in favor of revision—I asked him how many members he would be willing to lose in exchange for a new prayer book. "Ten thousand?" I asked. "Twenty thousand? A hundred thousand?"

"I hope we won't lose any members," the bishop replied, "but, if we must lose members, even as many as ten thousand, I will still support the new prayer book."

The new liturgy made its slow but certain way through committees and commissions and votes of bishops and deputies. But at Minneapolis, the site of the general convention in 1976, the prayer book was almost forgotten, overshadowed by a proposal to allow the church to ordain women to the priesthood. The motion to do so moved through the House of Bishops with much talk, and much apparent opposition, but when the vote came it was handily in favor of female priests. The House of Deputies took up the matter a night or two later in a debate that sometimes veered from considerations of theology to pragmatic arguments: Would ordaining women cost money? Would the church lose members? Mostly the talk was about justice. It was not right, many delegates claimed, to deny women anything that was available to men. The officer presiding ended discussion and called for a vote. When the president of the House of Deputies announced that the motion had passed overwhelmingly, the deputies stood and cheered and congratulated each other. They shook hands and patted each other on the back. Some women, a few of them already wearing clerical collars, came on the floor to be hugged, to have their hands raised in gestures of victory, to mount the platform while the deputies applauded. For Hal and for me and, in a way, for Jack, what happened to the Book of Common Prayer was no longer important. With the vote to ordain women, the Episcopal Church had betrayed its own past. It had violated almost five centuries of its own tradition.

Like most of our Nashville colleagues in the SPBCP, Hal and I were high churchmen; we called ourselves Anglo-Catholics. We educated ourselves with Roman Catholic books, the writings of Augustine and Aquinas, of Jerome, and, in my case, Francis de Sales. Hal read widely in the theology of the Greek Orthodox Church. After the vote to ordain women, we knew that we would leave the Episcopal Church, and we were virtually certain where we were going. My decision, which would not have been difficult in any event, was made easier by Jane's devotion to and admiration of some of the Dominican nuns with whom she worked at Aquinas College. She had seen in some of them examples of holiness, and she had learned some things about the church, its customs, its modes of operation, its inefficiencies that it somehow overcomes. She was ready to become a Catholic before the Episcopal Church ordained women. I was ready to do the same, but I loitered, wanting to make a quiet and, insofar as possible, invisible withdrawal from the SPBCP.

We were going to England late in the spring of 1977. One afternoon, a few weeks before we were scheduled to leave, I was sitting half clad on an examining table in my doctor's office, enduring the inconvenience of a routine physical examination. I was alone, waiting for the doctor to return, and it came to me that planes crash, cars wreck; foreign pedestrians in London often look in the wrong direction before they step into the street. It came to me, also, that I believed everything the Catholic Church taught. To stay out of the church, now that I had come to believe, would put my soul in peril. But what to do next? I had heard Jane speak of a priest who was confessor to the Dominican sisters. On my way home, I stopped by the Catholic Center where the priest worked and asked to see him. I gave my name to the receptionist, but explained that it would mean nothing to the priest. He did not know me. She suggested that I might want to tell her what I had come for, but I declined, and she did not press the issue; much of what happens between priests and their people must remain untold.

Father J. was a young man recently ordained; except for his service as a deacon, he had no parish experience. He assured me that God is "not unreasonable," that if Jane and I didn't survive our English vacation, our intention to become Catholics would be sufficient to save us from damnation. Having said this, Father J. paused as if he was uncertain what to do next. Finally, he took a thin and very simple catechism from his desk drawer and began to read aloud from it, asking me if I believed what the catechism said and if I had any questions. I did believe—that God had made the universe and had made all people including me; that I was created to love Him in this world and to share His eternal happiness in the next; that the "last things" as defined by the church were death, judgment, heaven, and hell. Neither he nor I used the word *eschatology.* Father J. appeared to be distressed by the very simplicity of our conversation. He was prepared to teach, to explain, but I had already been taught and required no explanations. When we had finished our perusal of the catechism, I asked Father J. if I could bring Jane to our next meeting. "No," he said, "let her come alone." She did, and as he had done with me, Father J. read to her from the same catechism.

As a teacher, I knew how Father J. felt. Good students will discuss whatever is open for discussion; they will enlighten their fellow scholars with comments and questions. Bad students often resist learning; they argue against whatever the teacher says. Teaching them is not as gratifying as instructing those who are bright, but their opposition helps to keep the class going. The worst students from a teacher's point of view are those such as Jane and I who agree without comment with whatever the teacher declares, who sit and wait for the teacher's next assertion. Should Jane and I have tried to help Father J. by asking questions to which we already knew the answers? Should we have engaged him with knowledge we had gained from more sophisticated catechisms, or from books we had read about Catholic theology? We were not afraid that we would embarrass him with our superior knowledge. He had recently graduated from seminary; he knew far more about everything Catholic than I. I kept my mouth shut because I didn't want to be the smart-aleck student who becomes an aggravation to the teacher. Jane, gentle by nature, was content to wait.

Father J. lived in the priest's quarters at a downtown parish. When we had finished our discussion of the small catechism, he suggested that we meet there and talk to the pastor, Father B. Father B. was older than Father J. He had experience working in parishes and dealing with converts. Soon after Jane and Father J. and I got settled in his office, he got to the point. "Why do you want to be a Catholic?" I didn't have to pause to think of an answer. I knew that, like the Episcopal Church, the Catholic Church had its dissenters: priests who preached against the dogma they were supposed to be teaching; lay people who declined to obey the rules of the faith and who demonstrated against the rules they would not obey. If the beliefs and customs of the Catholic Church had been promulgated by a House of Bishops and a House of Deputies, there would have been scant difference between Catholics and Episcopalians. I was fully convinced that the truth cannot be determined by plebiscite, that dogma cannot be eternally subjected to another vote that establishes another doctrine.

"I want to be a Catholic because of the pope," I said to Father B.

He was satisfied with my answer.

On the Saturday before we were to fly to London on Sunday, Jane and I were confirmed at the church where Father B. was pastor. Some of our Catholic friends came to see the job done. Some of the Dominican sisters from Aquinas College, still wearing old-fashioned habits and keeping a strict rule, came to welcome Jane into their religion. She and I confessed to Father J. We were baptized in case our long-ago Methodist baptisms had not been complete. We stood at the altar and made our profession of faith, our old friends Fannie and Lon Cheney, who were our godparents, standing beside us. They, too, were converts. Their godparents had been Allen and Caroline Tate, whose own godparents had been Raissa and Jacques Maritain. We were proud of our spiritual lineage.

Father J. did not drink, but he went happily with the Cheneys and Father B. and Jane and me to a bar in a nearby hotel, where we toasted our new religious affiliation. I thought of my old friend Randall Stewart, who had come into the Episcopal Church when he was several years older than Jane and I were now. He said that, when he got home from the confirmation service, he stood in front of a mirror looking for some physical change in his face or head that might have occurred when the bishop laid hands upon him. He found no sign, nor would Jane and I have found one had we looked. We didn't look. We finished packing our suitcases, counted our English money for the second or third time, and made sure that our passports would be ready at hand when we left the next morning. I never asked Randall whether he felt any different after his confirmation, and I did not ask myself any similar question. I was where I intended to stay for the rest of my life.

Chapter Seventeen

The Academic-Literary Life

As long as I was at Vanderbilt, the university grew. In the 1950s, after the veterans of World War II had graduated, year by year we admitted more students and hired more professors to teach them. We built dormitories to house them and classrooms where they could be taught. Sometimes enrollment went ahead of construction. The deans urged upperclassmen to find quarters off campus, which most of them were happy to do. The university bought buildings and houses adjacent to the campus and used those as temporary classrooms, although many of the "temporary" rooms were used for many years. I taught my large class in modern fiction for a long time in what had once been the auditorium of a church. One class, two or three students too big for the space assigned it, met in the bedroom of an old house; when the bedroom was full, somebody, more likely a man than a woman, sat on the toilet in the tiny adjacent bathroom, his notebook balanced on his knees. Faculty members shared office space. At Randall Stewart's instigation, we moved from our small offices in a classroom building to what had been the house on the small farm before the Methodists purchased the property and founded the university. The house was well built, most of the rooms were commodious, and if you weren't assigned a place in the windowless basement, Old Central, as Randall named it, was not a bad place to work. Cyrus Hoy and I shared a large upstairs room. Across the hall from us, Mr. Davidson had a room to himself, which he shared with Mr. Ransom for the term Mr. Ransom was with us. I moved into Mr. Davidson's office when he retired and shared it with Allen Tate, who met a seminar there.

One afternoon, one of Allen's students declared that what another student had said was "bullshit," which so upset Allen that, having reprimanded the miscreant, he dismissed class. His students retaliated by putting up a large sign near the mail room. "Allen Tate," it read, "is a tired old man." Allen was furious, as was I, but I suppose his late performance as a procreator disproved what the sign said.

I had never heard the words the student used in Allen's seminar or any like them spoken in a classroom. At that time, my writing students did not go beyond "damn" and "hell" in their manuscripts, but, as the student in Allen's seminar demonstrated, things were changing. Guy Owen, who regularly taught at North Carolina State, was a visiting professor for a year at the University of North Carolina at Greensboro, which at that time was open only to women. He said that the language in the manuscripts his female students wrote was more vulgar than any he had seen before in student manuscripts. He decided that if he asked one of the students to read her story aloud in class, she and the other students would be sufficiently embarrassed that they would clean up their language. But, he said, the girl read with great savoir faire, and he was the only uncomfortable person in the room. The proliferation of copying machines changed the way everybody taught writing classes. The students printed their stories before their classes met and distributed hard copies to their fellow students. Since the stories were no longer read aloud, the question of what kind of language students were allowed to use in their manuscripts was largely rendered moot. My students rejoiced in their new freedom. Some authors included words formerly unprintable in almost every line of dialogue, and it was hard to make them see that their expletives lost power when they were used too frequently.

I told my students an old Nashville tale of a lady born early in the nineteenth century who, insofar as her children and grandchildren knew, had never uttered an off-color word in her long life. To the shocked astonishment of her daughters, she said "damn" when she learned that her husband had been arrested and put in jail by federal troops that were occupying the city.

"Mama," one of the daughters said, "I never heard you use that word before."

"I haven't," the old lady said. "I've been saving it until I really needed it."

Whether my students took the point of my anecdote seriously, I do not know, but what we once considered indecent language was becoming common. Walking across campus, I heard snippets of conversation—not only dialogue among men of the sort to which I had long been accustomed, but the same kind of language when women talked to women and women talked to men. I knew that sooner or later this language would be used in my classroom, and I knew also that if I followed Allen's example and dismissed my students when an obscenity was uttered, I might as well not try to teach them. All I knew to do was to set an example. In discussing stories, we would examine lines or paragraphs, often reading them aloud. When a passage contained vulgarities, with the best humor I could muster, I would tell the students to read for themselves; although some of them read bad language aloud, most of them humored their crotchety old teacher.

One of a professor's duties in those days—and now, too, I presume—was to attend meetings of professional organizations: the Modern Language Association, which met in large cities during Christmas vacation, and the South Atlantic Modern Language Association, our regional organization, which usually met in Atlanta in November. We hired most of our new faculty members, particularly those who were just entering the profession, at the MLA meetings. We made appointments to interview candidates before we left Nashville. In New York or Chicago—wherever we met—members of the search committee waited in a smoke-filled hotel room and interviewed a procession of young men and women who were seeking jobs. In the early fifties, applicants enjoyed a sellers' market. Because of the war, there were too few Ph.D.s to go around. Good candidates had several jobs to choose from, and we did not always get the candidate we wanted to hire. There were weak applicants too—for example, a woman medievalist who could not read Latin. Most of the important documents, she told us, had been translated into

English. Another woman had written her dissertation on the difference between the ways men and women talk, the women furnishing more detail, the men anxious to get to the point. Some of my colleagues and I found this interesting, but only a department larger than ours could afford to offer a course on the ways in which women and men employ the language.

We asked the same questions of all the applicants: What were their specialties, which meant what were the subjects of their dissertations? What were their plans for future scholarship? Had they published, or had accepted for publication, any articles? Much of this was an otiose exercise. We had their dossiers before us, transcripts and bibliographies, if any, and letters of recommendation, the latter all but worthless, especially when the job market for beginning faculty became tight. Sometimes, two or more students who had studied under the same major professor applied for the same job. In many cases, the professor wrote separate letters of recommendation, each of which claimed that the student for whom the recommendation was written was the best student the major professor had ever taught. Only at funerals are more lies told than appeared in these flattering endorsements.

One of my earliest encounters with literary theory, which was becoming increasingly popular, was during the question period following a paper I read at SAMLA on a story by Flannery O'Connor. The question was filled with jargon that I did not understand, and of which most of my audience was as ignorant as I. A few others, who were professionally more au courant than the rest of us, knew enough to be angered by the question, and they reprimanded the young professor, who was intimidated, but not for long. Although we didn't know it at the time, his was the voice of the future. It was his jargon, his critical approach, that would survive, not ours.

When we had arrived at a meeting of SAMLA and our luggage was safely in our room, Jane and I would go to the hotel lobby to see what friends were already circulating there. We went slowly toward the exhibit hall where publishers displayed their books, and we went to the LSU Press booth, where we always found congenial company. For those of us who worked in southern literature, LSU was the press of record. Louis Rubin edited a series for it; the press published many of his books and books by Lewis Simpson and by Cleanth Brooks and by me. Les

Phillabaum, the director, and Beverly Jarrett, the editor in chief, were to most of us more than our publishers. They were our helpers, indispensable to our efforts to explore poems and novels written by southerners. Often our own books were shown at their booth and sold. Often we discussed books we might write with Bev or Les, and we went to lunch with them sometimes and sometimes we went with them to dinner.

These are some of the people who came to SAMLA, those to whom we talked in the hotel lobby or at the LSU booth or at publishers' parties that were always too loud and too crowded: George and Susan Core, Lewis and Mimi Simpson, Cleanth and Tinkum Brooks, Louis Rubin and — if he was attending the meeting — Hal Weatherby, with all of whom we went to dinner every SAMLA Friday night. Floyd Watkins and William Dillingham, both from Emory, came to the meetings. Floyd drank too much and had to be cared for sometimes, and he always told me how much he had disliked me when I was a beginning instructor at Vanderbilt and he was finishing his Ph.D. He assured me that he liked me very much now, but at one time I had been his Dr. Fell. Bob West, from Georgia, who had once been a sportswriter for a Nashville newspaper, usually came, often with Calvin Brown, a onetime Mississippi farm boy and friend of William Faulkner, a polyglot who could not only speak many foreign languages but could also name every part of a plow or a horse or a horse's harness. Also from Georgia was Bill Davidson, half brother of my colleague Donald Davidson, who almost never attended SAMLA and, unlike Bill, almost never drank. Bill in his cups was so amiable that all his friends wanted to take care of him, and he did not resist. On an ordinary SAMLA night friends who thought he needed to retire would accompany him back to his hotel. He never objected, but left his room again and went to another party. Sometimes others joined us, notably Hugh Holman, whose name comes to mind when I think of Walker Percy's title *The Last Gentleman.* Hugh may not have been the last, but he was certainly a notable example of trustworthy gentility. Whatever he told you was true to the best of his knowledge; whatever opinion he expressed was conceived in charity. Two of his colleagues, neighbors of his at Chapel Hill, had feuded until they stopped speaking to each other, but each was loath to conclude their argument. They communicated through Hugh, who carried their sometimes insulting messages from one to another with ironic good humor.

One night at a meeting of the Modern Language Association in Chicago, Hugh lingered in my room after others had gone to bed or, more likely, to another party, and we talked about religion—that most dangerous of subjects. We sought no conclusions and reached none, but the subject moved us toward considerations of good and evil. Prompted by films I had recently seen on television, I had been thinking of how ignorant I had been of what went on in Germany in the thirties and early forties. I wondered if my ignorance had been somehow culpable, although I knew that nothing I might have learned or thought would have saved a single life, much less altered the course of history. Hugh was ten years older than I, and he had probably been a better witness to what transpired in the world than I had been. I asked him what he had known about concentration camps and executions, and, for some reason, probably my deep respect for his integrity, I was comforted to know that he had been as ignorant as I.

Sometimes Donald Davie attended SAMLA. He had come to Vanderbilt from Stanford in 1978, and it seemed to me that as soon as he reached our campus other universities were trying to hire him. At one SAMLA I stayed up for most of a weary night to prevent a professor from Princeton from making an offer to Donald. Ten years after he had retired and returned to England he wrote me that he thought it was a shame we had not met until we had both reached late middle age, which flattered me and reminded me of how much his learned and witty presence had enlivened whatever group he favored with his presence. He was a good teacher, a good reader of his own work, a good poet. Like Allen Tate and T. S. Eliot, neither of whom he much admired, he believed that poems should be sufficiently obscure to require an energetic response from the reader, but, even though we were willing to strive to understand them, Hal and I admitted to each other that we didn't always know what Donald's poems were about. Sometimes I thought that he did not play quite fair. In his memoir, *These the Companions,* he mentions a woman with whom he briefly taught at a small college in Iowa. Later, in one of his poems, her name appears without explanation of who she is or how she came into Donald's life. You were out of luck if you hadn't read Donald's memoir. As time passed, poetry, both American and English, became more open, easier to understand, which was a development that Donald deplored. He felt, he said, that his work had been unjustly "marginalized." And so it had, but, I think and I think he knew, his poems were not ignored because of their obscure meanings but because of what they said. Unlike the poems of Philip Larkin, who had once been his friend and colleague in "The Movement," Donald's poems were grounded in his Christian faith. Near the end of his life, many of his poems were overtly religious.

Donald and I were good friends from the time we met, partners in conviviality, but I think, for several years, he hardly trusted my literary instincts and my ability to act on them. In 1983, halfway through his stay at Vanderbilt, he and I were at Sewanee to help celebrate Andrew Lytle's eightieth birthday, Donald to read a poem he had written for the occasion, I to make a talk in praise of Andrew. I could reminisce about drinking from Andrew's silver chalices, about going with him to hunt mushrooms in the woods, and about having observed his stern fidelity to his profession. Like that of Donald, Andrew's work was rooted in Christianity. Like Donald, he was faithful to his art above all mundane considerations, but, more than Donald, he deplored the course of events that had taken art out of its proper context and placed it as a separate entity in libraries and museums. After the birthday celebration, at the party at Rebel's Rest, the guesthouse at Sewanee, Donald took me aside for private conversation. It seemed to me that our relationship changed that night, an impression that was confirmed when Donald wrote from England that he thought of Rebel's Rest as the locus of our friendship.

Jane and I visited Donald and Doreen at their home in Silverton, an English town near Exeter with several pubs, a grocery store, houses with thatched roofs, and a church and churchyard where many of the crosses that mark graves are weathered and in some cases indecipherable. Donald liked the cemetery more than he liked the church, and I recall walking there with him with the same fondness that he remembered our conversation at Sewanee. The dead, most of whom have passed out of memory, have their own stories that engender speculation. When he visited Silverton, one of Donald's grandsons would ask Donald to take him to the cemetery and "read about the dead people," whose lives were doubtlessly enriched by Donald's reading. Hal and Louise and Virgil LeQuire and Jane and I urged Donald to return to Vanderbilt to lecture. He came in 1992 more reluctantly than we realized. He was seventy years old—still, it seemed to us, at the top of his game—but, in a letter to Virgil and Louise, he claimed otherwise. "Hal and Walter will never know," he wrote, "how much it cost me to return to Nashville." Hearing this Hal and I thought that he was simply being crotchety, which he sometimes liked to be, but three years later he had succumbed to cancer and lay with the dead whose stories he had read to his grandson.

Our Friday night group depended on George Core to seek restaurant recommendations from his friends in Atlanta, and sometimes the restaurants recommended were far away from our hotel—or were long drives whatever the distance. One Friday night our directions were to go out Roswell Road, but our cab drivers, who could not communicate with each other or with their dispatcher because their radios were broken, claimed to know a shortcut, and we were soon on one of the interstates. We had had a few drinks before we left the hotel. We were happy to be in one another's company; conversation flourished. Too late we discovered that the "shortcut" the drivers had followed was taking us beyond Atlanta, beyond where the restaurant was supposed to be. The happy effects of our booze were beginning to wear off, and those who had drunk little—Louis Rubin, who commonly limited himself to one drink, and Tinkum Brooks, who also practiced moderation—were very angry. Tinkum demanded to be taken back to the hotel, which assumed that the drivers knew the way back, possibly not a valid assumption. Louis issued the more practical demand that the drivers find a telephone, but this was sooner said than done.

We were in the country. Houses were far apart. Most of them were darkened, and even those where lights burned appeared to have been shut for the night. Finally, we found a closed filling station with an outdoor pay telephone. Either Louis or George called the restaurant, got new directions, and guided us to our destination—a nice enough country eatery where the staff had apparently waited for us more patiently than we had waited for our drivers to find their way. Most of us had another drink. Not Lewis Simpson, who did not drink at all; perhaps not Louis Rubin, who most of the time kept to his one-drink protocol. Tinkum had a martini, and her good disposition returned. It was her birthday—or close enough to it for her to have a cake and a candle or two. As often happens, time and memory turned our aggravating journey into adventure. After he got home, Louis Rubin wrote some funny doggerel about our long drive and the men who had driven us.

It seemed to me that the beginning of the end of our good times, the golden age for my generation of writers and critics and scholars, came not at a meeting of SAMLA or MLA, but at a 1985 conference to commemorate the fiftieth anniversary of the *Southern Review*. We gathered in Baton Rouge, where our hosts were the university and the university press. We gave papers and participated in panel discussions. Eudora Welty, Ernest Gaines, and Walker Percy read from their work, the first two from fiction already published, Walker from *The Thanatos Syndrome*, which was not yet finished. Robert Penn Warren read a poem or two before turning his book over to James Olney, then coeditor of the *Southern Review*, who read several more of Red's poems. Red would not die until 1989, but he was already weak from the cancer that would kill him. Ironically, Tinkum Brooks was also moribund, but she did not know it. Walking across the campus with Jane and Tinkum and Cleanth, I asked about Red, who was reluctant to talk about his own health.

"He's doomed," Tinkum said sharply, remembering as I did that his doctors had discovered his prostate cancer early but for some reason had not notified Red when there was still a good chance that they could save him. Tinkum, stricken with a tumor on her brain not yet diagnosed, would die before Red. Cancer would kill Walker in 1990—prostate cancer diagnosed too late, as Red's had been. Eudora would live on into a forgetful and painful old age and die in 2001. In spite of what I have just written, it would be wrong to say that I felt the shadow of death hovering over our conference. What I felt rather was a change in the atmosphere of the literary world, a confirmation of my sense at that SAMLA meeting decades before that our established ways of writing and reading, as substantial as they seemed, would be overtaken by new philosophies, new protocols.

At a panel discussion at the *Southern Review* conference, Houston Baker referred to Allen Tate as a "son of a bitch," an irony in view of Allen's strong response to improper language used in public. Baker was dredging up an old grievance. In 1932, Tom Mabry, later a friend of mine and then a member of the Vanderbilt English department, invited Allen to a party honoring James Weldon Johnson and Langston Hughes when the latter came to Nashville to read at Fisk University. Allen refused to attend the party and attempted to convince Mabry not to have it. His objection was that the party was being held in Nashville and was more a protest against social customs than a literary gathering. If it was being held in New York, Allen said, he would attend. In 1985, Allen had been dead for six years. Fifty-three years had passed since he had refused Tom Mabry's invitation, years during which opinions changed and attitudes softened. To judge Allen's past behavior by contemporary standards seemed to me then and seems to me now to be unfair. But this judgment of the past according to the perceived wisdom of the present became the almost universal modus operandi of the academic world. The work of "dead white men" was banished from the literary canon because their authors had been insensitive to issues of race and gender. Texts that weren't ignored were reshaped by the application of procrustean formulas; the writing was distorted, made to say what, in all probability, never crossed the authors' minds. The plays of Shakespeare were judged by standards of race and gender and sexual preference. All of Aristotle's philosophy was condemned because Aristotle sanctioned slavery. Allen Tate was not the only writer who was judged to be morally deficient by the standards of the modern literary world.

That night at dinner Jane sat next to Red Warren, who was deeply disturbed when she told him what Baker had said. For almost fifty years, Red had endured his own purgatory for the "separate but equal" philosophy that informed his essay in *I'll Take My Stand*. As his fame grew, he was interviewed with increasing frequency, and most interviewers began with questions that were not questions at all, but accusations of racism that Red again and again had to explain. As was the case with Allen, the self-righteous pursued Red beyond the grave. In his biography of Allen, Thomas Underwood dragged Red into his narrative, apparently his only purpose being to hold Red forever responsible for what he had thought and said seventy years before. Nothing Red had said or written since was considered.

In April 1987 twelve of us met in Chattanooga at the invitation of Cleanth Brooks to found the Fellowship of Southern Writers. There were Cleanth, Louis Rubin, Blydon Jackson, Elizabeth Spencer, Lewis Simpson, George Core, George Garrett, Fred Chappell, Shelby Foote,

Van Woodward, Andrew Lytle, and I. Others had been invited. Red Warren, Eudora Welty, Reynolds Price, Mary Lee Settle, Ralph Ellison, Jim Dickey, and others could not attend, but wanted to be counted as members of the fellowship, and twenty-six names were listed as founding members of the FSW. When we nominated Cleanth to be our first chancellor, he urged us not to elect him. "My name," he said, "is mud." But so were all our names. Literary theory in its various manifestations had gained hegemony in college classrooms, in the Modern Language Associations, national and regional, in textbooks, in literary magazines, and in the conversation of most professors and most critics and many writers. We who were founding the FSW were holdouts against the values and methods of our own society. Most of us had been raised on the New Criticism, and, although we too had arguments with our predecessors, we continued to value a poem or a story as a true rendering of what the writer meant to say. We believed that language could accurately communicate an author's intentions and that truth or an aspect thereof was available to those who were sufficiently gifted to find it. But as Cleanth had suggested, our beliefs and our writings, our very selves, were anathema to a large part of the literary world.

Cleanth was old enough to have seen the rise and fall of the South as a perceived source of a broad range of literary creativity. The profound novels of William Faulkner, serious in intention and sometimes difficult to understand, sprang from the same artistic impulse that had informed Margaret Mitchell's *Gone with the Wind*. As the struggle for racial reform advanced, respect for the South began to fade. Cleanth noticed that the American Academy of Arts and Letters, of which he was a member, increasingly elected to its membership writers from the two coasts. In spite of notable exceptions, such as Eudora Welty and Walker Percy, Cleanth believed southern writers were slighted, and he wanted the FSW to honor those writers who deserved honor and were denied it. We would offer prizes to southern writers, particularly to those who were starting their careers, but prizes cost money, of which the FSW had none. The Lyndhurst Foundation in Chattanooga paid for our first meeting, our travel, and our lodging. We met in the boardroom of the foundation. We invited influential citizens of Chattanooga to meet with us. But our reception by the citizens of Chattanooga was guarded, and the executives of the foundation made clear to us that our first meeting was the only meeting they would subsidize. Future meetings were up to us. But where would we get the money? We were writers, and raising funds was not an aspect of what we did.

The fellowship was Cleanth's idea, but from the beginning Louis Rubin was his chief executive, his point man. Louis helped to plan the structure of the organization. He helped choose the founding members. He had been on some of the literary programs organized every other year by the Chattanooga Arts and Education Council. He was a friend of the leaders of the A&E, who were anxious to work with the fellowship in an arrangement that would be beneficial to both organizations. Louis raised money to endow some of the prizes. Later other fellows—George Core, for example—found other sources of funds. George Garrett and Lee Smith established prizes that they personally financed. The Lupton Library at the University of Tennessee at Chattanooga set aside a room that would hold copies of books written by the fellows and, ultimately, archives consisting of correspondence among fellows, programs, minutes of meetings, and other documents that would be available to critics and scholars. Kurt Richter, a freelance photographer who then lived in New York, took pictures of the fellows that were hung in the FSW room in the library.

From its inception the fellowship offered prizes for poetry and fiction. Subsequently other prizes were added, for playwriting and nonfiction prose and for work within a specific category, such as a prize for writers from Appalachia. Many, perhaps most, of the writers who were subsequently elected to the fellowship had earlier won prizes from the FSW. Madison Smartt Bell, Josephine Humphreys, Jill McCorkle, Sam Pickering, Larry Brown, Kaye Gibbons, William Hoffman, Allen Wier, Bobbie Ann Mason, and Barry Hannah won prizes, as did others who later became fellows. The strong leadership of Cleanth and Louis was augmented by the work of George Garrett and George Core. For Cleanth, the fellowship was the fulfillment of a dream he had nourished and discussed with his friends for many years. When he died in 1994, he had appeared on programs sponsored by the FSW in 1989 and 1991. He had presided over meetings of the fellowship in our room at the Lupton Library. He had worked hard to found the FSW, but he had not worked alone. As I have said, Louis Rubin labored at his side, and Louis is so competent that he could have succeeded in any endeavor. Had he set out to make money instead of literature, we would all be applying to the Rubin Foundation for financial support. No record exists of what Cleanth or what Louis did separately or of what they did together. But the Fellowship of Southern Writers exists because of them.

In 1990, to my astonishment, my name appeared in Kingsley Amis's autobiography. One afternoon, Tom W., once my student and now a writer for the *Nashville Scene,* an alternative newspaper, called and asked for a response to what Kingsley had said about me. I should have gathered immediately from the tenor of Tom's question that whatever Kingsley had written had not been complimentary, but in spite of Jane Amis's attack on Nashville and Vanderbilt in the *Sunday Telegraph,* I had considered Kingsley my friend when he left Nashville, and I still thought of him as such. The last time my Jane and I were in England, I had tried to make an appointment to see Kingsley. Perhaps I should have suspected that all was not well between us when my appointment was declined. But I didn't suspect anything, and I had no idea what Kingsley had said in his book until Tom told me and later brought me a copy of the chapter in which I appeared. He said that my work was destined for the "dust bin of history," which was probably true. He castigated me for spending my leave from Vanderbilt in Nashville rather than in some more exotic location, claiming that my staying home proved that I was not a writer at all. There was nothing much to complain about so far: this was the sort of sniping that writers often engaged in. Then came perhaps the only charge that retains moral gravity in the modern world. He called me a racist.

There is no other accusation quite like that: none so completely deprived of the possibility of amelioration. You can be an adulterer, a thief, a murderer, any sort of villain that you choose, and there will be grounds on which you can modify your villainy—an unhappy childhood, an unjust society, the simple human weakness that we all share— but the designation of racism is absolute. Kingsley wrote that, at a dinner party at my house, I had said, "I couldn't find it in my heart to give an A to a Jew or a Negro." He wrote that some of my colleagues who were also present nodded gravely and seemed silently to congratulate me for saying something that they all believed but lacked the courage to articulate. The charge that I discriminated against Jews could easily be refuted by student records. I almost always had Jewish students in my writing classes, and many of them made As. But when Kingsley came to

Nashville, in spite of the university's continuing efforts, only a few African Americans were enrolled in the college. Of these, few majored in English, and, of these, very few enrolled in writing classes, no matter who taught them. Besides the lady who was the first black student in the college and who, much later, came to one of my book signings, I could remember teaching only two other black students. One was a graduate student who did make an A. The other was an undergraduate who made a C.

I knew the source of Kingsley's story. I had heard the line of dialogue that Kingsley had attributed to me as a part of an anecdote, told not at my table but at that of Russell Fraser. Kingsley had heard the same story at the same time, and perhaps then he had stored it away for future use against Vanderbilt and perhaps against me. I asked myself the eternal and eternally foolish question: why me? Had other members of the department been nicer to him and Jane—served them tastier food, poured them better whiskey? At first, all I could think of was that I had been a leader in the effort to get Russell Fraser to leave Vanderbilt. But there must have been other reasons. In her *Telegraph* article, Jane had judged Nashville to be backward, bigoted, and provincial—charges not totally without cause. She and Kingsley had charmed almost everybody who met them; they were entertained—often lavishly—by people who had lots of money, but who had read few books. Jane Amis had condemned all of Nashville. Kingsley was a better novelist than Jane. He knew that his piece would be most effective if he gave it focus by having one character represent the whole society, and I was it.

Dorothy Pritchett, Sir Victor's wife, wrote me from London that Kingsley had said bad things about many of his friends and then feigned surprise that they had been offended, saying he "didn't think they would mind." Before Dorothy's letter arrived, I heard from many people who had been in my classes years before. Many of them wrote letters to the newspaper extolling my virtues. Only one person, whose tenure at Vanderbilt had ended under ambiguous circumstances, suggested that my case ought to be investigated, but he and I had never met, and he admitted that he had never read anything I had written. The loyalty of my former students and my former and present friends turned what had been a trying experience into an occasion for good memories and deep gratitude. Kingsley seemed to have done me a favor after all.

Chapter Eighteen

A Time of Waiting

There was no proper waiting room in the intensive care unit at the university hospital in Columbus, but whoever was in charge of such things had done the best he could. In a wide space where two corridors met, across from elevators with busy doors, someone had laid a rug over the concrete floor and grouped some easy chairs, a small couch, and one or two small tables where those of us who had patients to visit waited for the scheduled time to go in. Tolstoy wrote that happy families are all alike, while each unhappy family is unhappy in its own particular way, but the group that lingered in the waiting area had their grief in common. There was the husband of a woman whom an intruder had hit on the head with a hammer. There were the parents of a young man who had been run over by an automobile and had not regained consciousness. His broken bones had not been set. For a while there were the parents of Peter, who had been with our son John when a pickup truck skidded on a snowy Ohio road and smashed John's red Subaru and John's face and body. Peter's younger brother had recently died in an automobile accident, and when Peter's parents learned that Peter was in the emergency room at Columbus, they were terrified, as Jane and I were terrified when we learned that John had been injured.

John, our youngest child, was on his way from Columbus to Gambier when the accident happened, and he and Peter were taken first to a small hospital in Johnstown. John had called us earlier from the Columbus airport where he had met Jim, another student returning from spring break, and we were relieved, believing that the dangerous part of his journey, the long drive on the interstate, was over. At first, talking on the phone to the nurse at the Johnstown hospital, I tried not to believe what she was saying. Nobody wants to hear bad news. No news is not necessarily good news, but we hold to the cliché because, between bad news and silence, silence is truly golden. Better not to know, better to return to the peace that prevailed before the phone rang, to the basketball tournament on television, players running up and down the court, Duke winning as usual. Did I say no to the nurse? Did I tell her I didn't believe her? I think not, but I clung to more hope than she had offered me. The doctor at Johnstown, she said, was trying to stabilize John, trying to get him ready to go by ambulance to Columbus, a trip that he might not survive, for the hospital at Johnstown was not equipped to treat him.

Jane and I knew very little about Columbus. We had been through there a dozen times, following the interstate across the city, remembering what lanes to be in, sure of our way when we turned off to go to Gambier. I had a vague idea where the Ohio State University was, but I could not have driven there without asking directions. The nurse at Johnstown notified us when John left her hospital, but we had no idea which way his ambulance took, what roads it would follow. Under better circumstances, I had tried to chart the course of loved ones who were traveling. When Pam and Gordon, our daughter and son-in-law, lived in Atlanta and came to Nashville to visit, I could say to Jane or to myself, "They're probably in Chattanooga now," and knowing how far it was from Chattanooga to Atlanta, we would know when to expect them to call if all went well. Now we knew neither distance nor direction, nor whether the snow would impede the way of the ambulance. Jane and I waited in our bedroom, longing for the phone to ring, but wondering, frightened of what news we would get when it did. We tried to talk, but we could think of little to say. We hoped that we would hear from John soon. We hoped that he was all right, still hoping against the truth that the nurse in Johnstown had tried to tell us. Finally, the phone did ring and the news was no better than what we had heard from Johnstown. John had survived the trip to Columbus, but the odds were slim that he would survive the night.

There was no direct flight then from Nashville to Columbus. We changed planes at Pittsburgh, where everything was off schedule because of the snow. We waited. We paced the airport concourses. We drank coffee. Finally, at Columbus, we rented a car, got directions, drove to the hospital, believing as I had allowed myself to believe from the beginning that the end of our journey would bring some ease to our agony, but this was not so. John lay on a bed in the intensive care unit, his body more still than I had ever seen it. With his head shaved, he looked very small, and the symmetry of his face and head was marred by the cuts on his scalp and face that had been clumsily sutured. A slender probe ran through his skull to measure pressure on his brain. Wires connected other parts of his body to the monitor beside his bed, which showed graphs and numbers, lines that peaked and fell, conveying information that Jane and I could not decipher.

Besides our sorrow and our fear, one of the things I remember most vividly about that time is the waiting. While John was in intensive care, we waited for the times that we were allowed to see him, once in the afternoon, once at night. Before we got to Columbus, a tracheotomy had been performed to make an entrance for the respirator, but we waited through surgery on his badly injured eye and surgery to restore his jaw and to repair other bones in his face and surgery to install a feeding tube in his stomach. There were other procedures—including an unsuccessful effort to remove a tooth that had been driven into his lungs—and there were several series of X-rays that continued until we brought John home. We waited in the Holiday Inn during our first days in Columbus when our fear was deepest and the doctors offered us scant hope. We waited later in a small apartment we had rented. We waited through the weeks alone and through the weekends with Pam and Gordon and our other son, Larry, who drove to Columbus after they finished work on Friday and returned to Nashville on Sunday night. And there were Father Ditto and Sister Lorna and Sister Mary John.

On our first Sunday in Columbus, Jane and I tried to attend mass at the Catholic center on campus, but the service there was ill suited to our feelings. We left and drove downtown to St. Joseph's Cathedral, which had been built a hundred years before and looked like the churches we were accustomed to seeing, and where the mass was said according to the way it was written. We were lucky that the mass to which we went was celebrated by Father Ditto, the pastor of the cathedral, who recognized us as strangers and listened to our story. A few days later he anointed John, and he was kind to us as long as we were in Columbus. Sister Lorna was kind to us too. She ran a bookstore in the cathedral undercroft that she kept open every day, even on Sundays for a few hours. Later, she told us that we looked deeply distressed when she first saw us; she wanted to help us, and she did help us by listening when we told her about John and offering sympathy that we knew was sincere and not simply a product of her good manners. She asked her friend Sister Mary John to pray for John because they both were named John and because she thought Sister Mary John's prayers were very effective. The hospital was in a questionable part of town, where few people walked after dark, but when John had been moved to a private room, Sister Lorna and Sister Mary John visited him at night, parking wherever they could find a place and walking as far as they needed to walk to get to the hospital. Jane told them that they were in a dangerous neighborhood and that they might be robbed. Sister Mary John said that she carried no more than a dollar or two in her purse and Sister Lorna did not carry a purse at all, so there would not be much point in robbing them. Jane was far from satisfied that they were safe, but the nuns seemed fearless.

We had no established relationship with a doctor at Columbus, no primary-care physician fully to explain to us John's injuries and the treatment he was receiving. Our doctors in Nashville told us that most of the doctors who treated John in Ohio were very skillful, but we rarely saw the neurosurgeon who was in charge of his case. Occasionally, we saw Dr. Miller's nurse-practitioner, who accompanied her on her rounds. The nurse baked a cake for us soon after we got to Columbus. She seemed to be truly sympathetic, but she thought John was going to die, and she wanted to be sure that his organs would be preserved for patients who needed them. The only doctors whom we saw every day were residents who had scant experience, but who were very sure of themselves. Like the nurse-practitioner, they thought John was going to die, and they told us so, once giving him only one chance in a hundred to live. But he survived to move to a private room, where Jane and I could sit with him and where his siblings could visit him on the weekends.

Pam and Gordon had met at the University of the South, where she was a member of the first class of girls to attend Sewanee. They had married at the end of her sophomore year. Gordon would bring her back to Sewanee later to finish her degree, but that was after John had left the hospital. Larry had attended Auburn for two years. During his sophomore year, for reasons I never fully understood, he decided to drop out of college, and to be sure that there would be no arguments over his decision, he skipped all his final examinations, got Fs in his courses, and was dismissed from the university. With one of his Auburn classmates, he spent a year as a bellman in a hotel in Fort Lauderdale before returning to Nashville and transferring to Vanderbilt. When John started Kenyon, Larry joked that John would be the only one of my children to finish college in four years, a failed prophecy that struck us both as ironic.

Many of John's classmates came from Gambier to visit him. We rented another small apartment to accommodate Larry and Pam and Gordon and where John's girlfriend could stay when her schedule allowed it. We tried to establish communication with John. Almost like the prophets of old imploring God, we asked John to make a sign, and finally he did. He squeezed Pam's hand when she asked him to. When we told Dr. Miller about John's response, she admitted that his coma had lightened, but she continued pessimistic about his chances for recovery. Gradually, he seemed to be awakening. Sitting in a chair, he turned the pages in magazines, not reading or even looking at the pictures, but going from one page to another as some part of his memory must have told him he should do. Because of his tracheotomy, he could not talk, but he could write, and later he did, his spelling and his grammar both correct. After he had been there for six weeks, it was time for him to leave the hospital. But how was he to travel to Nashville?

A hospital social worker helped us to try to make plans, but at first no plan seemed feasible. We had learned about helicopters from film clips of the Vietnam war, but a trip from Columbus to Nashville would require a helicopter to stop several times. The descent and ascent and descent again in an unpressurized cabin would impede John's recovery.

We tried to find a plane that would take him but failed, and the doctors said that his riding for eight hours or more in an ambulance was out of the question. When we had exhausted all our possibilities, help came from out of my distant past. Earl, one of my boyhood playmates, was now the commanding general of the Tennessee Air National Guard. Unknown to Jane and me, his doctor in Nashville was our doctor, and from our doctor he learned that Jane and I needed a way to bring John home. Earl decided to bring John home, but he would have to risk his own career to do so.

Regulations required that the Tennessee guard restrict training flights to the state of Tennessee. Earl assured me that he was going to take John from Columbus to Nashville, but, probably because he would be violating orders, he gave me few details. Again Jane and I waited. Impatient to know our plans, I called the airport that the national guard used at Columbus to be told that no plane from Tennessee was scheduled to land there, nor would one be allowed to land without the permission of Ohio authorities. We waited longer, as if waiting had become our occupation. Then a guard officer from Nashville telephoned to give us instructions in dialogue that would fit a made-for-television movie. We were to take John not to a military or public airport but to McDonnell Douglas, where we were to ask for Mr. Martin, who would tell us what to do. "Be on time," the voice from Nashville said. "We will stay on the ground long enough to get your son. But we will not cut our engines. If you are not at the airport when we get there, we can't wait for you."

The lobby of McDonnell Douglas was surreal in its austerity. A receptionist sat at a desk opposite the door. A uniformed guard stood beside the desk. There were a couple of large potted plants, but no chairs, no tables, no magazines. Whoever had designed the room had not expected visitors to loiter here. "Go back to your ambulance," the receptionist said. "Mr. Martin will come by in a blue Ford. Follow him."

I had hardly returned to the ambulance when the blue Ford appeared. It led us to another road, through a gate past other guards, and for another hundred yards to an airstrip. Here, one on each side of the road where it joined the runway, stood two men in plain clothes who carried submachine guns.

The nurse who had come with us stayed in the ambulance with John. I got out hoping to see Mr. Martin to thank him, but he and his Ford were gone. Once more, we were waiting, but not for long. Perfectly on time, a dull brown C-130 landed and taxied to within fifty yards of our ambulance. True to what the person in Nashville had told me, the engines were left running. Someone opened the rear entry to the plane, and an airman came to the ambulance, opened the door on the driver's side, and told the driver to get out. The driver, already impressed, as I was, with the mysterious Mr. Martin, with the road we had followed, the gates he had led us through, the armed men in plain clothes for whom vigilance seemed a habit, got out of the ambulance. The airman got in and backed the ambulance up to the plane, which seemed to be carrying a full crew: doctors and nurses who were commissioned officers; NCOs who were medical technicians; airmen, like the one who had taken over our ambulance.

Earl, his stars glittering on his shoulders, got off the plane. We hadn't seen each other for a long time. We hadn't gone to the same high school. We hadn't been in college together. I had known him when he came to visit his grandmother who lived two doors away from me. I had met him a couple of times soon after World War II when I was newly discharged from the marines and he was still in the air force, but that was years before. Would we have recognized each other had we met by chance? I think so. In any event, it was easy for us to spot each other in Columbus. He put his arm around me, which, I learned later, deeply impressed the ambulance drivers, who, understandably, respected generals more than they respected professors. Earl assured me that he would take good care of John. By the time we had exchanged a few words, John and most of the crew were aboard. Earl told me good-bye, and soon he was gone. The plane was in the air and on its way to Nashville.

John spent another six weeks in the Progressive Care Center at Baptist Hospital, and he did not like it. He was still weak, but he could walk almost as well as he ever could. With his tubes removed, he could talk and eat, but his mind was far from clear. He wanted to go home, and, if he was left alone, he would try to go. Once, when he had an incompetent sitter, he found the stairs at the end of his hall and went down a flight or two before an orderly found him and brought him back to his room. I think that he sensed that he was not well, that his mind was sufficiently clear for him to know that his thoughts were jumbled, and he believed that home, if he could get there, would heal the pain he sometimes suffered and repair his mangled thoughts. In addition to his mind, much of his body needed healing. Most of his front teeth had been knocked out in the accident. The tooth that had been driven into his lung remained there and would need to be removed one way or another. The surgeon brought into John's case by our internist recommended invasive surgery, but Jane and I believed that John had had too much of this already. We looked for an alternative procedure. We were home now, and we had friends on the medical faculty at Vanderbilt to advise us.

Jim, a pulmonary surgeon at Vanderbilt, would use an instrument that looked like a length of extraordinarily thin wire to go through John's trachea into his lung to grasp and remove the tooth. Jane and I waited in a small office next to the treatment room. We could hear Jim, his resident, and his nurse talking, but it was hard to understand what they were saying. John began to cough. Jim ordered a cough suppressant, and the coughing stopped. Jane and I were saying the rosary when Jimmy Sullivan, a young friend who had helped found the Society for the Preservation of the Book of Common Prayer, appeared and sat with us. Jimmy was now a student in medical school. He knew the jargon, and his ears were sharper than ours. We sat in silence, waiting once more. Then Jimmy said, "They got it!" He had heard the surgeon say this, but he sensed that Jane and I wanted to be sure. He went briefly into the treatment room and came back to tell us all was well. The tooth was out. Our prayers had been answered.

John had visits now from his own Nashville friends and relatives and from friends of Jane and me and of Pam and Larry. My mother had died five years before John's accident. Her younger brother was dead too, as were Auntie and Granddaddy, Puver and Popoo. B, my mother's younger sister, survived, but seldom left home. Aunt Janie, my mother's older sister, remained among the living and the mobile, as did her husband, Uncle Walter. With their daughter Jeanette to drive them, they came to see John, and on one visit Uncle Walter brought an enormous balloon to put on John's wall, an idea that was probably suggested by the large inflated sausage Pam had found for him. John imitates voices skillfully. Before his accident, he amused his family and his friends, including those in Ohio, by mimicking the backwoods accents of a girl on a television commercial who said, "Take home a package of Tennessee Pride." A few days before John came home, Pam saw in a restaurant a large balloon, the shape of a sausage, bearing the logo of Tennessee Pride. She could not get the balloon in the restaurant, so she went to the packinghouse and got a balloon for John there. Drawings and get-well cards and clippings from comic strips had also been put on John's walls. Even though John was beginning to remember how to read, every morning before he went to work Larry came to John's room and read the comics to him; together, they judged them good or bad, funny or ridiculous. Few were good enough to be posted on the wall.

John completed the physical therapy that the hospital provided. He could walk and dress and feed himself. He could build simple structures with blocks. But he was very weak, and he looked it. He was pale and skinny. Muscles were hardly visible on his arms and legs. There were gaps in his mouth where his teeth had been and deep scars on his face. The iris in his left eye had been removed. Small round scars were still visible on his head where his halo—a circular piece of metal from which thin wires ran to his nose and chin—had been attached after his maxilar surgery. A therapist at the hospital suggested that John lift weights. I arranged for him to lift at Vanderbilt, but, now that it was summer, the student weight room was closed. John worked with the varsity athletes. Three mornings a week, John and I entered a world of which neither of us had ever been a part, and we were received with charity. The strength coach found out how weak John was and told him which weights to lift and how to lift them. The football and basketball players alongside whom John worked learned his name and encouraged him. When he was ready to bench press a few pounds, one of the athletes helped him. When he was struggling, they encouraged him. "Come on, John," they said. "Come on, man, you can do it." Sometimes they applauded him. Finally, they spoke to him with the jocular vulgarity that they used with each other. They treated him as if he was truly one of them, as if, when fall and winter came, he was going to be with them on the field or on the floor.

His mind healed more slowly than his muscles. Perhaps if he had been in a sanitarium with people to work with him for hours every day, he would have made better progress, but mentally he had already gone beyond the expectations of the doctors and nurses at Columbus.

Dr. Miller's nurse-practitioner suggested that we talk to the parents of a young man who, like John, had suffered a severe brain injury. He was in the hospital when John arrived, he remained there when John left, and the doctors had not told his parents when their son might leave the hospital or what kind of life he could expect to lead when he left there. He had been at Columbus long enough for his hair to grow back on his once shaved skull, but he could not walk or talk, and sometimes he uttered loud meaningless sounds as his father pushed him along the corridors in a wheelchair. When Jane talked to his mother, she had no advice to give, nor could Jane offer her any words of comfort.

Misery is supposed to love company, but we found scant encouragement in the company of others who were miserable. The plight of the parents of the boy in the wheelchair aroused the sympathy that we had left to share, but mostly we focused on our own sorrow. Many people, all of them well-meaning, pointed out to us how much worse John's injuries could have been, a fact that we recognized, but such knowledge did not make our situation any easier. Our friends did comfort us, not by talking about John, but by kindnesses to us, sending letters and cards and flowers. Jane worked with John as much as she could, but his girlfriend with two companions had come from Kenyon to be close to him. The three girls rented an apartment and spent a lot of time at our house, time that Jane longed to have with John, to show him things and remind him of events in his past that might help jog his memory. But John enjoyed his friends, and they no doubt helped him to recover.

Little by little, he began to get well. Sometimes he was depressed. Once or twice, he threatened to kill himself. But he survived his own sadness, and, still looking abnormal, his eye not yet fitted with the colored lens that he would get, his missing teeth not yet replaced, he returned to Kenyon. His reception by the students was mixed, but, with the help of professors who had known him before his accident, he wrote his senior thesis on the novels of Walker Percy and graduated. With new teeth and the contact lens to cover where his iris had been removed, he spent a year in Paris, living with a friend, attending a course at the Sorbonne designed to teach French to foreigners. Later, he earned an M.F.A., working under Richard Dillard at Hollins. He earned certification as a teacher, and he is a regular substitute teacher in the public schools in Nashville. Some parts of his mind survived his accident. Other parts—his short-term memory, his practical judgment—continue gradually to improve, and I believe he can thank his family for that—not simply Jane and me, but his brother and sister and brother-in-law and their children.

A few years ago, I read a newspaper story about a man whose wife was bedridden and whose only child was confined to a wheelchair. Being of modest circumstances, the man, who expected to outlive his wife, worried about what would happen to his son when he died. I had been largely unmoved by the advice of acquaintances and of a few friends suggesting that I be comforted by considering others who were worse off than I, but this case touched my heart. I realized more fully than ever before how loyal Pam and Larry had been to John, and I felt great peace knowing that they would be near him and ready to help him after Jane and I were gone. In our family, we loved each other deeply, and that was what had sustained us. "The greatest of these is charity," Saint Paul wrote. In my experience this has been abundantly true.

Chapter Nineteen

Twilight Days

Because of a law passed by Congress that took effect on January 1, 1994, Vanderbilt could not force me to retire. I turned seventy on January 4, 1994, and I taught for five more years, growing older, doubtless teaching not as well as I had in earlier semesters. In my best days as a teacher, my classes were lively; students argued with each other and with me over the quality of whatever story we were discussing. They knew that there was no requirement that they agree with my judgments, but for the most part they did listen, and they did learn, and, according to their class evaluations, they liked me and liked the way I conducted our writing workshops. Some of them returned to take my classes a second time, which university regulations allowed for a few courses. I told Jane that when the students began to agree with me too readily and treat me with the respect sometimes given to the elderly, I would know the time had come for me to leave, and I would do so. But change is gradual; self-discovery is difficult; all I knew with certainty was that I was growing old. Occasionally, I would see a reflection of my timeworn face before I had had a chance to compose it for the mirror. Sometimes in class I looked down at my hands resting on the table, wrinkled and spotted, the knuckles arthritic; in addition—a symptom that I had not thought about when I was plotting my future at age seventy—some of the joy that being a professor had brought for fifty years was beginning to fade.

In my early days at Vanderbilt, I had many friends. I enjoyed attending faculty meetings and listening to what my colleagues had to say. I agreed with some of them and disagreed with others, and now and then I heard what I thought was a ridiculous remark, but we all respected each other, and we had a sense of common purpose: we were doing work of great importance; we were passing on to a new generation the foundations of our civilization that had been passed on to us, and if we were competent and fortunate, the books and articles we were writing and the research we were conducting might add to the common knowledge of our culture in some modest way. Now most of our discussions in departmental meetings were less about teaching and scholarship and more about changing the culture in which we lived.

We no longer hired to fill slots in traditional English courses. Now we were seeking to create a department that was in all ways politically correct. For example, there was only one openly homosexual person in the department—he had been arrested in a sting operation for propositioning young men—and my colleagues thought we needed more homosexuals, but, it turned out, they were difficult to hire. I was not a member of the interview committee, so I don't know what went wrong, but candidates accused the department of being homophobic or the dean of being homophobic and turned us down. Finally, a lesbian agreed to join us, but only if we gave a job to her partner. We did not debate whether we needed the expertise in literary study that the partner would bring. Rather, after our earlier rejections by candidates, we seized the opportunity to get two homosexuals at once, particularly since a lesbian who worked in our department earlier had gone to the University of Michigan.

I think many young scholars suffered culture shock when they came to Nashville and to Vanderbilt from more sophisticated venues. We hired a young woman to teach Asian American literature; she came to us from California and left after a couple of years. We had less trouble hiring African American professors than we had keeping them. Some of them did not like the pressure to publish in order to gain promotion, and two or three of them—including one I particularly liked and admired—

went to more relaxed situations. We also had trouble enticing students to enroll in the courses that some of our new faculty offered. There was not much demand for Caribbean poetry and fiction, but it was part of our arrangement with the newly hired teacher that the course be taught. Courses that had been among our standard offerings for decades lost some of their popularity. In the 1950s, 1960s, 1970s, and beyond, students filled auditoriums to hear Randall Stewart and, later, Dan Young lecture on southern literature, but the course was less popular when the reading list was revised. In one instance, the required texts, which would be the focus of class discussion, included only one novel and no poetry; the other books were focused on sociology and history.

I felt increasingly isolated in the department and increasingly separated from my colleagues. Some of them I respected and still do. Of some of them I was fond and still am. But the atmosphere in the department made me uneasy. It was not only alien to what I had always conceived to be our pedagogical mission. It seemed to me to be threatening to destroy the beliefs and institutions that had anchored my life. A year before I retired, I stopped going to departmental meetings, but my separation from the affairs of the department was incomplete. I received notices from the chairman. I was told what candidates were going to lecture on our campus, what the subjects of the lectures would be, and what credentials the candidates held that qualified them to teach at Vanderbilt, even though, most often, the choice of whom to hire had already been made. Requirements established by the federal government sometimes tainted our procedures. It seemed unnecessary but innocuous when, after we had hired a woman, we had to complete forms that proved that we had not discriminated against women in filling a job. It was worse, I thought, that we and many other institutions asked candidates to send vitae and bibliographies and letters of recommendation and invited them to come to our campus and lecture when there was no chance that they were going to be hired. It would have been better if we had hired the person we had decided to hire in the first place without raising the expectations of honest seekers of employment who had no chance of joining our faculty.

One day when I did meet with the department, a young colleague said that "sex had not been sufficiently theorized." I would like to say that I decided to leave at that moment, to walk out of our building and off the campus and be done with the whole enterprise, but such was not the case. I tarried for a few more months to hear of other subjects that needed more study by the theorists—gender, for instance, which in the minds of my colleagues was not the same as sex—and to hear the praises of diversity repeated at length. But finally I left. On a hot, Nashville, Saturday morning in June 2001, my son John, ever amiable, helped me to move. I had filled trash bags with papers I no longer needed. I had packed books in boxes, which I labeled according to contents. I had arranged with our custodian to borrow the departmental dolly, which obligingly he left out for John to use. The job would have been easier if I had followed Mrs. Vanderbilt's example and driven cross-country to the door of our building, but I lacked her panache. John hauled the books to our parking place and loaded them in the backseat and the trunk of my car. We were ready to go. I stood for a moment looking back at what I was leaving, and I was reminded of that other departure I had made fifty-five years before when I stood by the parade ground at Marine Barracks and gazed back at the neatly kept buildings, the flagpole with its flag lifting in an April breeze, and the house, now the home of the commandant, that the British had used as their headquarters in 1812. Then, I had wanted to go home. I wanted to get back to my vocation, to what I believed I was called to do. But I left with affection for the Marine Corps and with gratitude for the time I had spent in its ranks.

As I had done when I left the marines, on that Saturday morning in Nashville I paused to look back. It occurred to me, as it had before, that I had spent my life on this campus. I had come here as a freshman in 1941. I had returned in 1946 and once more in 1949, and I had never left again until now. Most of what I knew, I had learned here. Here, I had made most of my friendships that had endured through the years. If I had been leaving the same university, the same English department that I had joined when I left Iowa, the separation would have weighed heavily on my heart. Now I felt as if I was leaving a strange and unfriendly land where every value I cherished was under assault. I had left my keys to our building and to my office in the administrative assistant's mailbox. I had left a few books on my office shelves to be given to anyone who wanted them or to be thrown away. I never went back, never again entered the building that in a way had been my home. I kept my membership in the University Club. I kept the ID card that allowed me to use the library. I sold some of my papers to the Vanderbilt archives and gave the archivist some books: a copy of Allen Tate's *Mr. Pope and Other Poems* inscribed by Allen to Donald Davidson; a copy of Mr. Ransom's *Chills and Fever* inscribed to one of his prep school teachers; Mr. Davidson's personal copy of *I'll Take My Stand*. I was as sure as you can be in this risk-ridden life that the books would be preserved regardless of what happened to the university.

As a fiction writer, I had foundered for several years, writing something decent now and then — for example, a story that was included in the O. Henry awards for 1980 — but mostly I wrote criticism: *Death by Melancholy; A Requiem for the Renascence; In Praise of Blood Sports.* In 1995, I published a novel in which two of the main characters are old people, living on memories and enduring the misdirections of their failing bodies and faltering minds. By 1992 or '93, when I started writing *A Time to Dance,* many of my friends existed for me only in memory, and those who were still alive were an amusing lot. When I told other old people some of the funny things old people did, nobody was offended. It was all a part of what we had to go through. My two old characters were based on Lon and Fannie Cheney, Jane and my friends for many years and our godparents in the Catholic faith. Given what I knew about their behavior, I was helped in their own creation. But, for me, the old people alone were not strong enough to carry the book; I needed young people to play against the old and to develop the basic theme of the novel in different terms. These characters I had totally to invent, which made my work harder.

The two old characters, Max and Bunnie, had been great sinners in their time, but they had outlived their lurid pasts and were now faithful Catholics. The young female character, Shannon, was a Catholic as well, but she no longer went to church, and she was deeply at odds with her parents and all that her parents had tried to teach her. Julien, the young male character, would have called himself an agnostic had he thought about it, but his mind seldom turned to religion. The theme of the novel, as I conceived it, was love and redemption and the mystery of both. The public conflict is the struggle over abortion, which is partially conveyed by Shannon's pregnancy, but it is never stated overtly. I thought, and still think, that the book succeeded, as did most of the critics who reviewed it. Writing for the *New York Times,* Penelope Lively complained that in England there were too many television shows about old people, and she was tired of the subject. But none of my novels sold well, and Penelope Lively had not spoiled my chances to have a best seller. Rather, I had written my Catholic book decades after the work of Catholic writers—Flannery O'Connor, J. F. Powers, and the others—had been popular in this country. As had been the case with my writing about the South, my timing was off. I had come too late to the Catholic renascence to entice large numbers of readers.

After *A Time to Dance*, I wrote short stories, these Catholic also, the characters all convinced, some more than others, of the Christian mystery, the life of the world to come. A major difference between novels and short stories is that, most of the time, stories evolve in a private world. The characters react to each other, love or hate each other, are in conflict, which is the sine qua non of all fiction. Novels require a public dimension, a conflict in which the world at large, or as much of it as possible, is engaged and impinges on the private conflict in which the characters are involved. Some short stories have public conflicts, as novels do, and some of these are the best that have been written in our language. The private tension between Gabriel and Gretta in Joyce's "The Dead" develops within the larger conflict over Irish nationalism. The distant war and the immediate influenza epidemic enhance the love story of Miranda and Adam in Katherine Anne Porter's "Pale Horse, Pale Rider." But there is scant public action in Eudora Welty's "A Worn Path" or in Henry James's "The Beast in the Jungle." In my stories—"Only the Dance," for example, and "Bare Ruined Choirs"—the only aspects that you could consider public action are mysterious and undefined. What passed in my stories for public action was metaphysical.

I would have been happy finishing my career writing short stories. But years ago I had promised my daughter, Pam, that I would write the story of my life—or as much of it as I could remember before I died. I delayed, but when I developed melanoma, I could delay no longer. My melanoma began with a lesion on the back of my neck that I wouldn't have noticed if it hadn't left minute spots of blood on my pillow. It was removed and identified by a dermatologist, and then more tissue was removed by an oncological surgeon, and the glands surrounding the original lesion were found to be free of cancer. For a year, all was well. Then a routine X-ray revealed a spot on my lung. The melanoma had spread and was now incurable. I got the news about myself in early

November 2003, from the surgeon. At that time, during the few minutes that it took, it was perhaps harder for him to tell me my prognosis than it was for me to hear it. He couldn't look at me. His eyes wandered about the room, peering at everything, but maybe seeing nothing. He fully understood the gravity of his message. He had said what he was saying now many times before. It was his job to speak of death, and he did not like it. He told me that I would live for eight to fourteen months, during which I would feel fairly well. My last illness would come suddenly and be short. He was sorry.

The doctor left the examining room. His nurse, who had left the room when he had come to give me my prognosis, now returned and told me how sorry she was for me. She suggested that miracles happened, cures were found: I might live for a long time. She hoped I would. Did I thank her? I don't remember. Like the doctor's eyes, my mind drifted, turned away from reality. Jane had her own doctor's appointment that afternoon. Not wanting me to be alone if the news was bad, Pam had gone to the doctor's office with me. We walked to the parking lot, dark now that the sun had set, and it was easier than I could have dreamed it would be to tell her what the doctor had said. Only at the end did my voice tremble. We got in our cars and left, but I still had Jane to tell, and that would be harder. I got home before she did. I waited in my study, sitting in the chair she had bought me, thinking, but not thinking. Letting the thought of my impending death penetrate my mind.

I heard her car coming up the driveway and went to meet her at the door. She may have guessed what the doctor had told me; she may have seen it in my face or in the way I was standing. We hugged each other.

"It's bad," I said. "It's very bad."

I could say no more. Neither could she. We held each other and cried. When I could speak again, I told her I was sorry. We had been married for fifty-six years. Now we would soon have to part, and the idea of parting filled us both with sorrow. As usual, we had a drink—in my case more than one. We had our dinner as usual, but I don't remember what I was thinking or what we talked about. I had long said that I didn't want to live into a protracted old age. I feared disabilities that led to nursing homes more than I feared dying. I clung to that notion, but if I had had a choice, I would have lived a little longer and, perhaps, found a more convenient time to be told that I was going to die.

Chapter Twenty

Timor Mortis Conturbat Me

Medical theory holds that at first cancer patients deny to themselves that they are mortally ill. I fought against doing this, I think successfully. I had seen the spots of blood on my pillow. I had seen the X-rays and the scan results and the reports of the pathologists. Now and then, for reasons that I do not know, I would suddenly think that my case had been misdiagnosed or that a cure for melanoma would be found, but I quickly put these thoughts aside and forced my mind back to realities. Knowing that I was going to die was a burden that Jane and I lived with. For me, the burden was heaviest when I thought of the future, and I was surprised to learn how much of my life I had lived in anticipation of what was to come. There had always been something to wait for, in fear or in hope: growing up, finishing your education, going out into the world. When you were in love, you looked forward to marriage, and, whether you were in love or not, everybody in my generation waited for the end of the war. So it went on, the births of children and the deaths of relatives, sometimes after long illness. I waited anxiously to see my books in print and to get promoted and to try to solve the problems of my life and those of my children's lives. Always, for me at least, there had been something to come, and now my impending death was the only future that I could depend on. But I make this sound worse than it was—or is, since I'm still alive and writing.

I don't know whether knowing that I was going to die concentrated my mind as Dr. Johnson said it would. I do know that an aspect of what the existentialists had written was true for me: realizing that I did not have long to live made me conscious of the goodness of life, of the beauty of the world, created and natural, and of the love of my friends and my family. Some of my days were very happy, but sometimes they were melancholy as well, made so by the belief that I was doing something for the last time. I was convinced, wrongly as it turned out, that Christmas 2003 would be my last Christmas on earth and that January 4, 2004, would be the last birthday I would celebrate. In the spring, Jane and I went to our house in Florida. Driving over the causeway that led us toward the Gulf of Mexico, I thought that, when we crossed the causeway going back to Nashville, I would have spent the last days I would ever spend on the beach. This may have been true. We have not been to Florida since, but, when we were there last spring, I was able to accommodate myself to my future. I do not know what caused me to get angry, but I very well remember that I spoke sharply to Jane, saying that I probably would never come to Alligator Point again, asking her, without saying so, to be sorry for me and to humor my whims and my moods. It would be foolish to say that I was healed by my anger, but a day or two later I remembered that for everybody in the world there is a last time to do everything. When we drove back over the causeway, I looked at the sunlight sparkling on the water and felt no pain.

At the end of Hemingway's *For Whom the Bell Tolls*, Robert Jordan, injured beyond possibility of escape, waits to die. He does not believe in any life beyond the present. He knows that some other people do believe, and he wonders whether it is easier for believers or nonbelievers to face death. The first time I read this novel, I was a believer. It seemed to me that dying would be easier if you thought of it as a transition from one life to another and not as a finality, but I was young and strong. My future seemed limitless, and I did not give the question Robert Jordan asked much thought. One of my colleagues in the English department whom I liked and admired for his learning told one of our secretaries that he was not an agnostic; he was an atheist. He was certain that there was no god, no spiritual father to whom we could appeal at times of danger and difficulty. He died of prostate cancer after being sick and suffering a good deal for a long time. Nobody that I knew of asked him whether his cancer and all its ramifications moved him to change his mind about the existence of God. I think that cancer could move you in almost any theological direction. Ivan Karamazov said that he would not believe in or worship a god that allowed little children to suffer, but why stop with children? Why believe in a god who allows you to suffer or even one who allows cancer to exist?

This logical question is asked by most of us at one time or another, and its logical answer is not to believe. I surmised that my colleague died not believing because he tried so desperately to live. For several months, I took an experimental drug that doctors hoped might cure or retard the growth of my melanoma. I took one white tablet a day, but this was a very powerful tablet, and it produced many side effects, all of them unpleasant. The drug seemed also to have some effect on my melanoma. When I started taking it, I had three lesions on my lung—one small, one medium sized, and one large. The small lesion disappeared, the middle-sized lesion did not grow, but the large lesion continued to get larger. It might have been even larger if I had not taken the drug. Concerning cancer therapy, there are many mysteries. I think that my atheist colleague's lack of faith caused him great suffering. To the end of his life he submitted to whatever therapy, some of them quite painful and debilitating, would offer any hope of making him live longer. Another of my colleagues, a close friend, told me that he enjoyed smoking and that he was willing to shorten his life to continue to smoke. But smoking caused a cancer on his bladder. Radiation then caused an abscess that could be cured only by surgery, and no surgeon would operate on him because of his emphysema. He lived for several months in great pain.

With no future to indulge, no plans to be made for the years to come, the dying person finds that the terms of life are modified by the prospect of leaving it. The main character in *Living in the Present*, a novel by John Wain, decides at the beginning of the story that he is going to kill himself, but, before he does, he will settle some old scores and do some things that he was afraid to do when life lay before him. Of course, after he does a few bad things, he decides that he doesn't want to die after all, thus establishing the comic tension of the novel. I have no old scores to settle. Most of my old enemies are dead, and I can think of nothing that I want to do that would earn the disapproval of the priesthood or the constabulary. You do outgrow your sins, as Saint Augustine said and did. Except for moments of impatience and annoyance, which do not last long, I think I behave myself properly. But the ancient joke about the man who is so old that he won't buy green bananas is valid. I, too, have stopped buying many things: new clothes, books to replace those I sold when I retired, a new computer. I will not buy another car. If we ever have a plasma television screen, Jane will buy it. On the other hand, I wanted to buy some things for our house, and with Jane's help—and concurrence—I have bought most of them: new outside doors for the den; new outside lights; new light fixtures for the bathrooms. I wanted to get new plumbing fixtures for Jane's bathroom, but Jane didn't want to get into that, and I succumbed to another brief fit of anger. As was the case when we were at Alligator Point, I felt the rush of time. I believed my impending death authorized me to do whatever I wanted to do and obligated Jane to help me. But I saw that that was foolish too, and I tried to detach myself from the things of this world and to think of another dimension of reality.

Detachment from the palpable world was Prince Andre's mode of dying. In the time of the action in *War and Peace* almost two hundred years ago, everything, sometimes even death, was accomplished in a leisurely fashion. Prince Andre removed himself emotionally from the loved ones who sat beside his bed. Every day the distance between him and them grew as he made his passage from one life to another. If God gives me sufficient strength, I want to imitate Prince Andre. My colleague the atheist took an opposite course. He acted on the advice of Dylan Thomas and struggled mightily against "going gentle into that good night." Robert Louis Stevenson wasn't a good poet, but his intention to "lay me down with a will" sets a good example. I am able now to cherish my little epiphanies that followed my anger about Alligator Point and about Jane's plumbing fixtures. Eliot wrote in *Four Quartets* that "all we know is what we don't know." I wonder if it is also true that the important things we do are what we don't do. Or is detachment itself an action?

We know that our experience of the night is different from our experience of the day—a statement so obvious that I apologize for making it. Night is a time of fear, of foreboding; night is when ghosts walk. Creatures that hide in the day come out in darkness. Night is also the time when many people think of death, and, in one way or another, most people fear it. Those who knew him best said that Philip Larkin feared death mightily. In his poem "Aubade," he wrote of awakening in the deep darkness of night and of being afraid of dying. His fear was absolute. He was more than disturbed or distressed. Although he does not put it in these terms, darkness for him was the color of death. His fear was assuaged only when he saw the first light of dawn outside his window. I wake in the night too, but I find darkness no more threatening than daylight. Lying in bed, waiting to go back to sleep, I usually think of whatever I am writing, of where I left off the day before, of where I'll try to start in the morning. But, of course, I do think about death in the night. In a country music song, the singer claims to think of his estranged lover only once a day—"All day long, once a night from dusk to dawn." It would be wrong for me to say that I think of dying all day long, but when I wake in the morning my first thought is of my impending end. It comes as the return of a memory—not as something I've forgotten, but as something that I must keep in mind.

In the literature of war, usually in the memoirs of soldiers, we read of men who foresee their own deaths and predict them on the night before the battle; but there are too many variables in play here to make the predictions meaningful. In battles many people die, and no one counts those who say they are going to die and then live. Apparently, their failed prophesies are soon forgotten. Andrew Lytle said, "You must know when you're going to die." Andrew was then in his eighties, and I had just told him the story of a friend whose sick father called him at his office to say he was dying. When my friend reached his father's house, he met the doctor on his way out. The doctor assured my friend that there was no change in his father's condition. "He's not the one who is dying," my friend's father said, and an hour later he passed away. In the weeks before Andrew died, he lay on his bed for good parts of the day and sang hymns. A few days before he died, Jane and Hal Weatherby and I went to see him. He lay on a couch across from the fireplace, and, with what must have been a great effort, he tried to reprise his customary hospitality. From his couch, he welcomed us, asked us to sit down, offered us drinks. This was a few days before Christmas and a few days before his birthday on December 26. I reminded him that his mother had said that he came into the world "like a wet firecracker."

Andrew laughed. "You remember that, do you?"

It seemed to me that, unlike Prince Andre, who was one of Andrew's favorite fictional characters, Andrew was not withdrawing from life, but reaching out, struggling not so much to live but to maintain the customs by which he had lived. A few days after our visit he died.

Preparing to die is complicated, even for people of modest means and simple habits. A few years ago, in an effort to avoid estate taxes and the expense of probating our wills, Jane and I divided our assets and put half in a living trust for her, half in a trust for me. Not long after, Congress changed the amount of taxes to be paid on estates, the amount to grow smaller every year until for one year there would be no tax at all. Then the law will expire and Congress, ever hungry for money, will probably pass a new law, and the fight with the IRS will start all over again. Ah, I am tempted to think, by then I will be, as Randall Stewart used to say, "Mercifully under the sod." True, but Jane will probably still be here, and it is mean-spirited of me to rejoice when she will have to suffer. Experience should have taught me more than I seem to have learned: nobody avoids the troubles of life; as long as you're alive, you must endure them. Being moribund will not excuse you.

My older son, Larry, who is our executor, asked me to write my obituary and to plan my funeral. I did. I named my pallbearers, chose the music. But no eulogies. I mentioned earlier that more lies are told at funerals than are included in letters of recommendation. At the funeral of a woman I had known long and well, one of the eulogizers praised the deceased for her gentleness, her kindness, her charity toward all. But I knew that the woman had been as mean as a snake. While she lived, she did not leave a wake of happiness behind her. Everyone else at the funeral must have known what I knew, but there was no way to redress this web of falsehoods. For one of us to rise and challenge the veracity of the eulogizer would have been a greater breach of charity than any the dead lady had perpetrated, but it was hard not to feel morally involved somehow, somehow culpable. After the funeral of a truly good woman, our bishop said, "They say we are sending everybody directly to heaven now, but So and So was certainly saintly." But was she saintly enough to skip purgatory? I did not raise this question with the bishop.

One of my Protestant friends, to comfort me when he heard of my diagnosis, said that dying was "like walking through a door." I could tell by the way he spoke these words and repeated them more than once that he was quoting someone else, and I think he was pleased by this image, but there is no authority—Catholic or Protestant—for it. Some people have had visions of the world to come. There are many testaments from those who have had "near-death experiences," who have been physically dead for a short period and then come back to life. They claim to have gone briefly to a happy place, but they do not say much about the landscape of heaven. Saint Paul knew that whatever vision of the hereafter he had had was fragmentary. Saint Thomas Aquinas apparently saw more. He denigrated all the brilliant work of his life after his heavenly vision.

Now, as I come to the end of my life, I am tempted, as many people are and have been, to think that some times in the past must have been superior to what we are now enduring. I am not thinking of storms and earthquakes, of fires and floods and volcanic eruptions, all of which are bad, but of the loss of faith that seems to be endemic to the Western world. In the last century, both Romano Guardini and Jacques Maritain said, although not in the same words, that the devil had made such a spiritual shambles of what used to be Christendom that living in what remained of Christian civilization would soon be bearable only for saints. It is easy to agree with this judgment and to be depressed by it, but those parts of the mundane world that depress us are part of that from which we must separate ourselves, part of the detachment that is an aspect of death. Detachment is not easy. I know that I am going to die. I have lived longer than I was given the right to expect, but my interest in what happens around me has hardly waned. I watch the news on television while I cook breakfast; I read the morning paper while I eat. From time to time, I must remind myself that I will not be here for the next political campaign, or for the next football season, or for the election of the next pope. In spite of John Donne's claim that the death of a single person reduces mankind, no one besides those who know and love me will realize that I am gone. Sometimes as I drive on West End Avenue I think: on the day of my funeral the traffic will continue to be heavy; stores will continue to do business; the pharmacist will still fill prescriptions; conversation will still flourish in the barbershop. In speaking of the wholeness of mankind, Donne was referring to a mystery that, like the mysteries of the rosary, is ultimately unfathomable to most human minds.

Although I have claimed to be somewhat loyal to it, clearly I have not followed Prince Andre's example. I have not detached myself from the mundane aspects of my life, but I can think of them more easily and with less regret at leaving them than I could a year ago when the idea of death was new to me. My doctor gives no advice about dying. He asks me whether I am suffering certain physical symptoms. He asked me once if I was depressed. I told him no and that I didn't intend to become so, which he must have considered a naive answer. I wait. Eliot advises us to wait without hope or love or faith, but *Four Quartets,* he said, is a poem "about the experience of believing a dogma," which I take to mean that it is a poem about living and not about dying. Whatever it is about, I judge the advice the poem offers as too stringent for me to follow. I discern in the subtle questions asked by friends their desire to know what moving toward death is like, but I cannot tell them. My physical debility could almost as well be a sign of old age as a symptom of cancer. My consciousness of my coming death is perhaps no more acute than that of any sensible person who has endured beyond his valid expectations. Willingly or not, I follow Eliot's advice. I wait. But not without faith, not without hope, and, I hope, not without charity.